keeping a rabbit

keeping a rabbit

emma magnus

For over 60 years, more than 50 million people have learnt over 750 subjects the **teach yourself** way, with impressive results.

be where you want to be
with **teach yourself**

Illustrations by Barking Dog Art.
Photographs courtesy of Eric Gaskin, *Fur & Feather* magazine.

For UK order enquiries: please contact Bookpoint Ltd, 130 Milton Park, Abingdon, Oxon, OX14 4SB. Telephone: +44 (0) 1235 827720. Fax: +44 (0) 1235 400454. Lines are open 09.00–17.00, Monday to Saturday, with a 24-hour message answering service. Details about our titles and how to order are available at www.teachyourself.co.uk

For USA order enquiries: please contact McGraw-Hill Customer Services, PO Box 545, Blacklick, OH 43004-0545, USA. Telephone: 1-800-722-4726. Fax: 1-614-755-5645.

For Canada order enquiries: please contact McGraw-Hill Ryerson Ltd, 300 Water St, Whitby, Ontario, L1N 9B6, Canada. Telephone: 905 430 5000. Fax: 905 430 5020.

Long renowned as the authoritative source for self-guided learning – with more than 50 million copies sold worldwide – the **teach yourself** series includes over 500 titles in the fields of languages, crafts, hobbies, business, computing and education.

British Library Cataloguing in Publication Data: a catalogue record for this title is available from the British Library.

Library of Congress Catalog Card Number: on file.

First published in UK 2006 by Hodder Education, 338 Euston Road, London, NW1 3BH.

First published in US 2006 by The McGraw-Hill Companies, Inc.

This edition published 2006.

Typeset by Transet Limited, Coventry, England.
Printed in Great Britain for Hodder Education, a division of Hodder Headline, 338 Euston Road, London, NW1 3BH, by Cox & Wyman Ltd, Reading, Berkshire.

Hodder Headline's policy is to use papers that are natural, renewable and recyclable products and made from wood grown in sustainable forests. The logging and manufacturing processes are expected to conform to the environmental regulations of the country of origin.

Impression number 10 9 8 7 6 5 4 3 2 1
Year 2010 2009 2008 2007 2006

contents

acknowledgements

Without Anne McBride, Georgie Hearne and David Appleby none of this would have happened and I will be forever grateful for their inspiration and teachings.

I would also like to thank Anne Mitchell, Owen Davies, Anna Meredith and Mairwen Guard for their valuable comments and contributions, as well as *Fur & Feather*, the Rabbit Welfare Association, the British Rabbit Council and the Association of Pet Behaviour Counsellors.

Above all, I have to thank my parents for introducing me to the joys of keeping un-neutered rabbits in a garden colony when I was a child and Patricia Gaskin for re-awakening the interest in my mid-twenties.

Although not a thankyou, the rabbits I have kept over the years, including Pumpkin, Swede, Parship, Lentil and Porcini, deserve a mention as they have taught me many things that helped me understand their relatives whilst allowing me to road test products, tips and accessories.

Last but not least is Dan, who makes everything possible.

introduction

Rabbits are the third most popular pets in the UK today with an estimated 1.1 million living in or out of the home. We have a unique relationship with the rabbit that does not exist with any other domestic species. We have treasured the rabbit as a food source for centuries, worn it as a coat or footwear, loved them as a child or adult's pet, protected the countryside by trapping and shooting them, running them over in our cars, exhibited them for their fur and looks, used them for research, created much loved cartoon characters, poisoned them with Myxomatosis and introduced them into our home as house rabbits.

There are now some 65 recognized breeds of rabbit in the UK, ranging in body size from the tiny Polish rabbit to the large British Giant and the coat colour has changed from the grey-brown of the wild rabbit (known as agouti) to a diverse array of whites, oranges, blues and reds. Some elements of the rabbit's shape may have changed – particularly in relation to the ears that can be in proportion and upright, through to very small or very long and floppy – but the rabbits that we keep as pets today are all related closely to the wild ones that we see across Europe and in Australia.

Sadly rabbits are one of the most misunderstood species, with an estimated 33,000 being put up for adoption each year. Many of these owners have not understood the needs of this complex prey animal that can live for at least five years and requires more than a daily bowl of food and a weekly clean out.

what is a rabbit?

In this chapter you will learn:

- **about rabbit physiology**
- **how rabbits interact with other rabbits**
- **how rabbits live in the wild.**

Before we look at whether a rabbit is for you, where to obtain one, what it should be fed and where it will live, we need to learn about the rabbit as an animal to fully understand its needs and appreciate its nature.

A brief history

Compared to our dogs and cats, which were domesticated a very long time ago, people only started to keep and breed rabbits in cages about 1,500 years ago. This makes the rabbit a relative newcomer to the pet scene, meaning that much of the domestic rabbit's behaviour and lifestyle is exactly the same as that of the wild rabbit.

Rabbits make good pets because they are naturally:

- sociable – living in groups and interacting with others
- adaptable – able to live in a variety of situations
- complex – with specialist breeding and parenting behaviours
- appealing.

However, they can make a challenging pet as they are also:

- a prey animal – prone to fearful behaviours, such as aggression
- a scent communicator – using their urine and faeces to mark areas of territory
- destructive – causing damage through digging and grazing
- interactive – requiring regular social contact and exercise.

Many people think that a rabbit is a rodent, like a guinea pig or rat, but the rabbit that we see in our fields is the European rabbit, *Oryctolagus cuniculus*, and is the closest living relative of our pet rabbits. *Oryctolagus cuniculus* is a member of the order Lagomorphs, family Leporidae. Other members of this order include the hare and the American Pika (also known as a 'rock rabbit').

Rabbits originated in southern France and Spain and are herbivorous prey animals that consume large quantities of vegetation and are preyed upon by a range of predators such as foxes, stoats, weasels, badgers, hawks, dogs, ferrets, cats and humans. When they make up such a large proportion of the diet of so many animals, it is amazing that any survive, let alone live in such great numbers!

The day-to-day life of the wild rabbit is a constant battle for survival and much of the rabbit's physical appearance and behaviour patterns have evolved to aid its survival whilst helping them to exploit their natural environment.

Rabbit physiology

The skeleton

Rabbits have a very fragile skeleton with elongated bones in the lower back and back legs to enable hopping. They have very powerful back legs that help them run fast and protect themselves but they can damage their spine if they kick or stamp too hard.

The coat

The fur of the wild rabbit is dense with a brown-grey colour on top with a white belly and tail. The soft undercoat is covered with guard hairs that are longer, stronger and provide an outer coat.

The body colour of the rabbit has evolved to avoid detection in low light levels whilst the white tail is thought to provide a flash of white as the rabbit runs that signals to other rabbits to return to their nearest burrow entrance.

Rabbits moult once a year, usually starting in March and shed their coat starting from the face, along the back and over the rest of the body. The warmer winter coat has usually developed by October.

Under their chin, rabbits have a sub-mandibular gland that produces a colourless secretion. This is wiped onto items within the territory and individual members of the group by the high-ranking male to spread a 'communal scent'.

Rabbits have a flap of skin under their chin that is very obvious in some females. This is called the dewlap and is the area where fur is plucked when they are making a nest for their young.

The digestive system

The area where rabbits originated was dry scrubland but rabbits were able to survive and increase in numbers on this almost indigestible food source through some special adaptations in their digestion.

Rabbits spend much of their time out of the warren grazing selectively and this can account for five or six hours of the rabbit's day. When the food passes into their digestive system, it is sterilized and then separated into nutritious and non-nutritious particles. The non-nutritious particles are passed out of the body as dry, hard droppings. The nutritious particles collect in a large sac between the large and small intestine called the caecum where they are fermented with bacteria and processed into soft smelly droppings (known as caecotrophs).

As these pass out of the rabbit's anus the rabbit reaches round and consumes them (known as refection) and then they are digested again to produce the harder droppings that we find deposited in fields and hutches. These droppings are high in a form of nitrogen that fertilizes the ground as the rabbits graze ensuring that plants will grow within the territory and keep the rabbits well fed in the future.

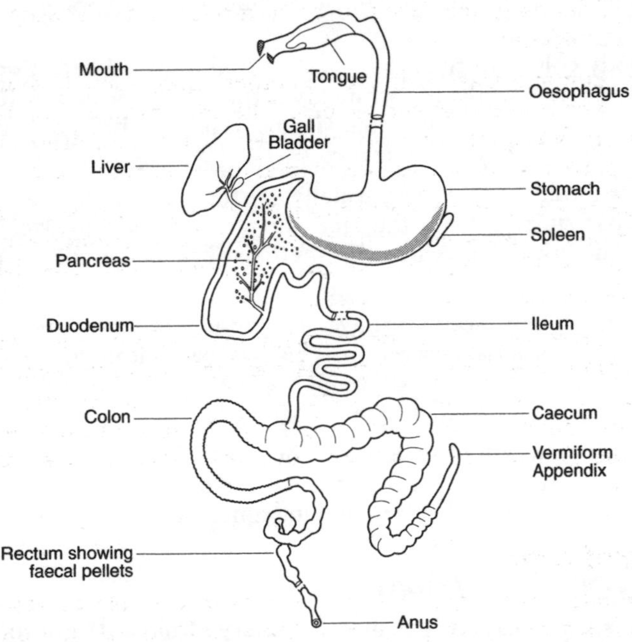

figure 1 digestive system of the rabbit

This sensitive digestive system relies on a diet high in plant fibre (for further information see Chapter 04, Nutrition).

Urinary system

Like most mammals, rabbits have two kidneys and pass urine out of the body through a tube called the urethra. Normal rabbit urine may be clear or cloudy and often contains calcium carbonate crystals as rabbits excrete any excess calcium.

Secretions from a gland called the inguinal gland (situated in pockets either side of the genitals) enable male rabbits to mark inanimate objects and individuals with their urine during courtship or territorial disputes.

Respiratory system

Rabbits always breathe through their nose and only breathe through their mouth if they are suffering from a severe respiratory infection or some form of distress. Their nostrils are slit and can be opened to increase the rabbit's sense of smell by drawing the scent over a moist area allowing a greater absorption.

Rabbits communicate with each other using smell, body postures and some discreet sounds. The increased use of the sense of smell is common in prey species that cannot afford to alert predators to their presence by making too much noise.

The rabbit's sense of smell enables it to quite literally sniff out danger. Scent is also used as communication between individual members of the rabbit's group, enabling them to live underground with no natural light.

Odorous secretions are deposited within droppings, urine and through chin rubs. Urine, droppings and chin rubs are used for marking all around the territory, and large latrines full of droppings can be seen on the edges of the territories. Urine sprays and chin rubs can be used to mark individuals within the group.

Ears and eyes

Wild rabbits have large, concave ears that are able to move independently giving very accurate hearing. Their ears are also full of blood vessels that help them to regulate their body temperature by varying the amount of blood flowing through them. When a rabbit is warm, more blood flows through the ears thus cooling it as it goes near the surface before being transported back around the body.

Eyes are positioned on the side and towards the top of the head enabling the rabbit to see ahead, to the side and behind. The rabbit is long-sighted so it has good distance vision and tears that are drained away through tear ducts lubricate its eyes.

Teeth

Young rabbits are born with a set of teeth that are shed between three and five weeks of age and replaced with a permanent set of 28 teeth. These comprise of two upper and lower cutting teeth (incisors), two 'peg' teeth (that sit behind the upper incisors to stop the lower incisors pressing onto the upper gum) and 22 grinding teeth (molars).

Rabbit teeth grow continually throughout their life and can only be worn down by long periods of time spent grinding and chewing tough vegetation.

Legs and feet

The back legs of the rabbit are very well muscled to enable them to run very fast and to pack a hefty punch if they are caught. The long bones in the back legs also allow rabbits to stand up

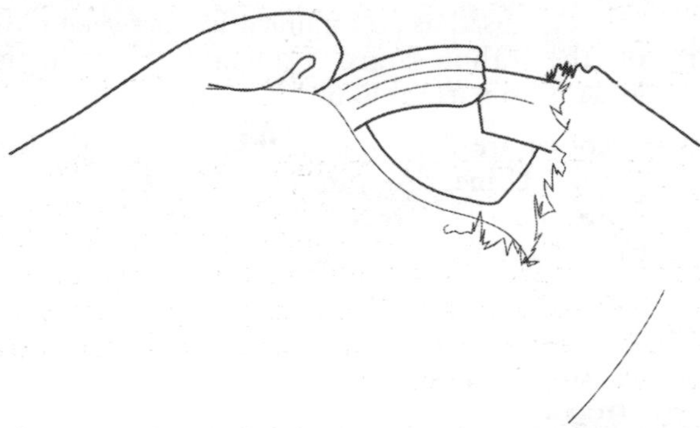

figure 2 rabbit's upper and lower incisors

and survey the area for predators, but this added height is also helpful for getting to hard-to-reach bits of vegetation.

The shorter forelegs have five toes and the longer back legs have four. The undersides of rabbit's feet are hairy to aid insulation and to help them grip on slippery surfaces. It is also thought that the hair acts as a shock absorber if the rabbit is running fast on a hard surface.

Reproductive system

The analogy 'breeding like rabbits' is absolutely true. In a single breeding season, a female rabbit can produce 30 babies. Of course, not all of these individuals will survive to adulthood (in fact very few wild rabbits live over one year of age) but the chances are that the population size will still increase dramatically.

Females (known as does) reach sexual maturity when they are about three and a half months old and males (bucks) when they are four months. A female rabbit is a reflex ovulator, so she ovulates in response to a mating and can be pregnant again within a day of giving birth.

Each testicle of the male rabbit is situated in the scrotum that is attached to the rabbits' lower stomach near the top of each back leg. The testicles descend at around 14 weeks of age but can be withdrawn back into the abdomen outside the breeding season and during times of stress.

The breeding season starts in January and continues until July/August, with a seasonal peak in spring. The gestation period of the rabbit is around 30 days and an average litter size is five.

Towards the end of her pregnancy, the doe rabbit finds a suitable dry spot for her nest and digs a slightly sloping tunnel about 2 m (6½ feet) long with a single entrance. The 'room' at the end of the tunnel is lined with a nest made of grasses and fur from her chest and stomach. The young, called kittens, are born hairless with closed eyes and the mother blocks the entrance to the nest each time she leaves.

The mother rabbit visits her babies for just five minutes every twenty hours, the rest of the time she engages in the normal activities of eating, resting, socializing and grooming. This form of parenting is called absentee care and is very rare among domesticated species, making the rabbit quite unique in this respect. Absentee care probably evolved as a defence against predators – the best chance the mother can give her babies is to keep them hidden and draw as little attention to them as possible.

The kittens start to emerge from the nest when they are about three weeks old, and are weaned six days later. They will start producing their own litters within twelve weeks and are fully grown at nine months, if they have survived that long.

Social behaviour

It's not just physical factors that help rabbits survive; living in groups benefits the individual, as many pairs of eyes and ears are better than one. If a threat is spotted the rabbit alerts other members of the group by thumping its back legs and this signal sends members of the group scurrying for cover.

Rabbits live underground in warrens, which consist of interconnecting burrows with many junctions and several entrances. The location and design of the rabbit's home has evolved to reduce the chance of predation – if a rabbit is followed into a burrow it has a chance to evade the predator by changing direction, rather than getting trapped in a dead end.

The depth and complexity of the warren requires a group of individuals to dig and maintain. The density of the earth that the rabbits are digging may dictate the size of the rabbit's group – the number of individuals appears to be smaller when the ground is softer. The protection that a well-designed and maintained warren provides may be a causal factor for the social lifestyle of rabbits.

Exclusively the females dig the tunnels whilst the male rabbits often watch or scrape small areas of ground. The female digs with her front feet and then pushes all the loose soil away with her back legs.

A large warren may house over a hundred rabbits, with stable family groups of two to fourteen members within. It is thought that adult rabbits rarely leave the group in which they first breed, and females tend to stay with their litter mates, although juvenile males are encouraged to migrate away from their birth group by adult males. These males will integrate into another group outside the breeding season. The larger the group the more females, and all members defend the territory from rival groups.

There is a hierarchy, or pecking order, between the adult males of the group that helps to maintain order, whereas females tend to live in a state of mutual acceptance outside the breeding season. During the breeding season, females will fight (sometimes to the death) for access to the nesting sites that are situated away from the main warren.

As noted earlier, faecal pellets are used to mark out territories and rabbits rub their chins over prominent items within the territory to smear them with secretions from the scent gland located under the chin. Once a pecking order has been established, higher-ranking male rabbits may 'chin' lower ranking males to maintain stability. 'Chinning' also helps to identify members of the same group as they will all share a common smell.

Higher-ranking males mate with the females during the breeding season and will guard them from other males. Males literally 'wait their turn' and mate with a female of similar rank to them. Although females ovulate in response to mating they are only sexually attractive to the males every seven days so each rabbit should get a chance to mate successfully several times during a breeding season.

When rabbits greet each other, the more subordinate individual will crouch down, appearing smaller and non-threatening to the higher-ranking rabbit. Allogrooming, or grooming each other, is often observed between individuals and is a comfort behaviour that helps to strengthen relationships.

Urine contains odorous gland secretions and can be a useful method of anointing areas within the territory as well as individuals in the group. Part of a male rabbit's courtship ritual can involve the practice of enurination – spraying urine onto a female. A high-ranking male rabbit may also urinate on a lower ranking male in a combative manner.

Any aggression within the group tends to be between members of the same sex. During the breeding season, female rabbits are more aggressive than males but males will respond to invading rabbits or another male approaching their mate.

The aggressive behaviours that rabbits may exhibit prior to any direct conflict include chasing, leaping, bouncing and paw scraping. Rabbits often run parallel to each other before any encounters to enable each rabbit to work out the relative size of the other individual and decide if the conflict is likely to end in his or her favour. These behaviours ensure that many disputes are resolved by non-violent confrontations.

Feeding

The majority of a rabbit's life is spent feeding – it is estimated that some 70 per cent of the time that a rabbit spends outside the warren is spent gaining food. The rabbit is most active during the twilight hours of dawn and dusk – a cooler time of the day with the added advantage of some camouflage from predators.

Grazing wears down the incisor teeth that grow continuously throughout the rabbit's life and provides the rabbit with the opportunity to feed selectively ensuring that it eats a diet high in plant fibre.

When rabbits first come out of the burrow they keep their heads down and feed quickly, with breaks to check for predators. As all members of the group are behaving in the same way there is a fair chance that any danger will be spotted. After some time, the grazing becomes more casual with the rabbits zigzagging to select the best bits.

Communication

As we have already seen, the majority of communication that takes place between rabbits is limited to smell. This is yet another anti-predator device and serves to prevent the rabbits drawing any attention.

Rabbits rarely use sounds to communicate but the visual signals used to communicate with each other include moving the ears, changing the position of the tail, affecting their way of walking and increasing tension in the facial muscles. A relaxed rabbit is likely to be lying on its side or front with its back legs extended, or sitting up with its ears back against its head. A scared rabbit, which is unable to run away, will crouch down and make itself seem as small as possible with its eyes appearing to bulge out of its head. A lower ranking or submissive rabbit will also crouch down but avoid eye contact.

Using the back leg to thump is one of the few sounds that rabbits make. This is used at times of potential danger to alert other members. Tooth grinding and grunting may be associated with aggression but a rabbit that is grinding its teeth whist sitting hunched up is probably in pain. A rabbit that is in immense pain or fear may scream, an awful sound that probably lets other rabbits know of the immediate danger.

In summary

- Rabbits are prey animals.
- They have a specialized digestive system and are herbivorous (vegetarian).
- Rabbits communicate with each other using body postures and smell but have good hearing.
- They are very social, living in groups.
- Rabbits are most active during the twilight hours of dawn and dusk.
- They have teeth that grow continuously and have to be worn down by grazing.
- Rabbits are highly fertile and ovulate in response to mating.
- Their breeding season is January to July/August.

02 is a rabbit for me?

In this chapter you will learn:

- **whether a rabbit is for you**
- **what a rabbit needs**
- **about rabbits and children**

The decision to own a rabbit is not one that should be taken lightly. Taking on a pet involves commitment over many years and it is morally wrong to take on an animal without exhibiting a duty of care throughout its life.

There is a terrible human tendency to buy pets on a whim – in response to an advert, after passing a pet shop or after we have spent time with a friend that has a pet we would like. Whilst some very responsible people have bought animals this way, the majority of purchases would be better made with a prior understanding of the animal and its needs.

Remember, there are thousands of rabbits sitting in rescue homes waiting for the right person to take them home. Many of them will never be homed again. Rehoming your rabbit because 'it didn't work out' is irresponsible and passes your failing onto another person.

Should I have a rabbit?

To you see whether you are suited for rabbit ownership, ask yourself these questions:

- Do I have surplus income each month to cover food, housing and veterinary care?
- Am I prepared to spend at least an hour per day with my rabbit for the next five to ten years?
- Do I have enough space for a rabbit hutch and is there room for a rabbit to have some exercise?
- Will I check his teeth and nails regularly, groom him every day and clean him out every few days for the rest of his life (five to ten years)?
- Is there someone who could look after my pet if I have to go away?
- Am I interested in understanding my pet's behaviour?

If you answered 'no' to any of these then you may not be suited to keeping a rabbit.

If you answered 'yes' to all of these questions then you may be suited to keeping a pet and should now spend some time deciding on the breed of rabbit that you want, where you are going to get it from and how you are going to keep it.

What does a rabbit need?

To ensure that your rabbit is healthy, happy and makes a good pet, you must provide all of the following:

Exercise

Rabbits are naturally very active animals and do not respond well, both mentally and physically to a lack of exercise.

In addition to the correct size hutch, regular access should be given to an area where the rabbit can hop and skip around with few limitations. An enclosed run incorporated in the lower level of a two storey hutch or as a separate facility on the lawn is ideal, but an enclosed garden can also allow the rabbit some supervised exercise.

Good nutrition

Rabbits have evolved to consume large quantities of low-quality food stuff, such as grass and they therefore require a diet that is high in fibre and low in sugars. Feeding a balanced natural diet will help to prevent digestive disturbances, dental problems and destructive behaviour. Nutrition is covered in greater detail in Chapter 04.

Housing

All housing should be large enough for rabbits to stand up on their back legs and take several hops in any direction. Remember that the housing that meets these criteria when the rabbit is young may not be the right hutch for them once they are fully grown.

There is no hard or fast rule as to where a rabbit should be kept. There are however, many considerations to take into account before making a decision and, of course, that choice can change at anytime in the future.

Rabbits are reasonably destructive, similar to many other pets. Before bringing a rabbit into the home time must be taken to ensure that the home is prepared – also known as 'bunny proofing' (see Chapter 06). If such measures cannot be put into place then it may be better to keep the rabbit in an enclosed area within the home or outdoors with a companion.

There are some behavioural problems that are caused by boredom and are more likely to occur in rabbits that are kept outside in a small hutch. If the rabbit is to live outdoors do ensure that it is given access to an area large enough to give exercise and complex enough to give the rabbit some stimulation.

When rabbits live within the home it is easier to monitor their health than if they are being kept outside in a hutch. Outdoor rabbits must be thoroughly checked on a daily basis by removing them from the hutch, checking them over and then watching them carefully as they hop about. It is not easy to ascertain overall health and welfare by peering into a small, low hutch once every few days, so take the time and make sure the hutch is as big as you can afford.

Social contact

Rabbits are social animals and need regular social contact every day. If you are planning on keeping a rabbit in your home then it is feasible that you will be able to provide all the contact that it needs, assuming that you don't work long hours. If a rabbit is going to live outside then your ability to provide regular social contact in this environment needs to be considered.

Of course, it is better to obtain a pair of rabbits and then they have each other but problems can arise if the wrong decision is taken as to the sex of the individuals.

The combination of rabbits least likely to cause problems is usually a male and female pair. Putting two females or two males together is likely to develop into competitive combat in territorial situations during the breeding season. Many rabbits suffer severe injuries as a consequence of these pairings and many more are separated permanently.

The obvious problem with a male and female pairing is unwanted pregnancies but neutering should be performed on young male rabbits as soon the testicles have descended or the rabbit starts to display sexual behaviour. Neutering females that are not intended for breeding also helps prevent the development of uterine cancers.

Something to remember is that having one rabbit makes their relationship with us very special and very strong bonds can develop between the rabbit and owner in these situations. Having two or more rabbits may mean that they become less interested in us once they have members of their own species to interact with.

Health care

Rabbits require regular vaccinations against the diseases Myxomatosis and VHD (for more information on these diseases see Chapter 10). At this time, your veterinary surgeon will give your rabbit a health check to ensure that there are no problems with their teeth, ears, eyes and digestion. On a weekly basis, you should also be prepared to spend the time checking your rabbit to enable you to pick up any problems at an early stage.

Pet insurance

Some companies now offer pet insurance for rabbits and these policies can help with veterinary fees but do not usually cover annual vaccinations. They are worth considering if you are concerned that you might not be able to cover the costs of any major treatment but, with the average excess in the region of £35 (US $64), you might also wish to consider putting the equivalent amount in a savings account with a good rate of interest.

Rabbits and children

It is very common for children to be given a pet rabbit in exchange for the dog or cat they really crave. The feeling amongst parents is often that rabbits represent an easier alternative, a pet that will involve less care and expense. In addition they are readily available at most pet shops and can come home that day with their home, food, bowls and brushes.

Unfortunately for many children the relationship falls at the first hurdle with the pet 'not doing anything' or becoming aggressive, because it is scared. With a rabbit living for five to ten years the purchase of these animals, especially for a child who may lose interest, should be as a result of an informed decision.

Rabbits are very sociable but they are prey animals and have a very different perspective on the owner–pet relationship than our fellow predators, the cat or dog. The interaction between a human and a prey animal involves an enormous amount of trust and can very easily descend into distrust and fear. The greatest issue affecting a prey animal's relationship with a child is handling. Each breed of rabbit differs in size and husbandry needs. Some of the larger rabbits are too heavy for a child to pick up; some of the smaller breeds are too small for hands that may squeeze too tightly.

I do not recommend the rabbit as a child's pet but I am perfectly happy for an adult that has a child to own a rabbit. If you have a young child, buy a large rabbit so that they can stroke it but not pick it up. If your child is a bit older (and wiser), picking out a rabbit that is not too scared or confident and making sure that your child is handling the rabbit correctly can prevent problems. For more information on temperament and handling see Chapters 06 and 07.

The responsibility for a pet must always lie with the adult. To do otherwise, risks a child losing interest and a rabbit on its own in a hutch at the end of the garden.

Rabbits and other pets

Some rabbits co-exist quite happily with our other pets but there are numerous rabbits that have suffered bad injuries, or worse, from dogs and plenty of guinea pigs that have been bullied by their companion rabbit.

Keeping a rabbit involves understanding its status as a prey animal with dietary needs and behaviours specific to that species. Dogs and cats are predators and may develop an unhealthy interest in your rabbit – particularly when it is young. Dogs can chase rabbits backwards and forwards through the wire of the hutch whilst cats can stalk small breeds of rabbits. If a dog has lived happily with a cat in the past, or another rabbit, then there is a fair chance that it will accept the new arrival. If they have no experience of other pets, particularly small furry ones, then you need to consider the practical consequences of this. Is the rabbit going to be continually hunted? Will you be able to give your rabbit some social contact and exercise safely? Is your hutch and run secure and dog-proof? If your rabbit is going to live in the home – how will you keep them separate? At the end of this chapter there is a step by step process for introducing a dog to a rabbit which should work for most dogs, although some (particularly those that have had experience of chasing and killing small animals) may not respond as well as others. Even with the most placid of dogs it is not recommended that the dog and rabbit be left unattended, just in case.

Cats don't tend to engage in long periods of chase and are used to hunting small prey, so they usually accept the presence of a rabbit, in or out of the home after some gradual introductions using a secure indoor cage or outdoor run for the rabbit.

Rabbits and guinea pigs

The idea of keeping rabbits and guinea pigs together is not new. There are many people who have successfully raised a pair through to a colony of many individuals with no problems. But the risk of a problem is high and the victim is usually the smaller guinea pig. The success or failure of a pairing with a rabbit is dictated by the housing, space, the hormonal status of individuals, the behaviour and health of the rabbit.

In the wild, guinea pigs live above ground on grassland and move around through tunnels created in the grass. Most rabbits and guinea pigs are housed in hutches with very little space or 'furniture'. In this situation, there is little option for escape so a guinea pig is unable to diffuse a situation by hiding or communicating (as both species communicate differently). When people pair a guinea pig and a rabbit, they often choose same sex individuals to prevent expenditure on neutering. An entire male or female rabbit can mount a guinea pig, quite avidly, for long periods of time and cause injuries. Similarly a rabbit that becomes territorial around the time of puberty may direct that aggression onto the guinea pig.

On a practical note, guinea pigs have a different dietary requirement to rabbits as they are unable to store Vitamin C and must be fed a special supplemented diet. In addition, many rabbits carry the bacteria *Bordetella bronchiseptica* with no signs of illness but can infect guinea pigs with this respiratory disease.

Colonies of guinea pigs and rabbits, kept within a large enclosed area can work. In this situation every animal becomes accustomed to the behaviour of the other species from a young age and has members of its own species to interact with. If problems occur in this environment there is less chance of injury, because of the increased space and options for avoidance.

Method for introducing a dog to a rabbit

- The first step in this process is to teach your dog the 'leave' command – 'leave' means don't chase, look at me and don't eat.
- Take some of your dog's favourite food treats and hold one between your finger and thumb. Offer it to your dog and as

he comes near the treat, remove it by closing your hand, at the same time say 'leave'. Then open your hand and let him take the treat saying 'have it'.

- Repeat this process until your dog does not try to investigate the food when it is offered but is happy to take the food once given the command 'have it'.
- It is important that your dog has grasped the basics so try to practise this stage in various locations, at various times of the day to be sure that the command has been learned.
- The aim of the next stage is for your dog to learn to leave a titbit in one hand but take a nice reward from the other. Put your hand with a treat in it, out to one side of your body. Ask your dog to 'leave' and, when this happens, praise and offer a really nice treat from your other hand which is in your lap. Your dog should quickly learn to keep focusing on you to receive a really nice reward.
- As you will need to gain your dog's attention when there is the distraction of a rabbit around, you should now repeat the previous stage using a variety of means to get your dog to look at you, rather than the food. You can do this by creating a diversion such as coughing or making another noise. As soon as you get your dog's attention, praise, say 'have it' and give the titbit.
- Keep repeating this stage and gradually increase the time that your dog waits for the titbit.
- Once you are at this stage of the exercise you should train your dog to leave non-food items (it is easier to start with boring objects and build up to your dog's toys). Put some fairly unexciting household objects on the floor and as the dog investigates them, say 'leave' – when your dog looks at you, praise and give a very tasty reward from your hand in the lap saying 'have it'. Remember only to give the reward when your dog has ignored the objects because you gave the command.
- Practise this exercise using more interesting items and then repeat on walks, remembering to treat each time you successfully command 'leave'.
- The final stage for the 'leave' command is to ask your dog to pay more attention to you than a person. Use a friend or family member as a stooge and ask your dog to 'leave' them when they enter the room. If this is successful then next time the person can behave in a silly manner and again, your dog

is asked to 'leave' and given a treat for succeeding. This stage needs to be repeated with several people in a few locations until you are confident that your dog will leave anything to come to you for a really nice treat.

You are now ready to introduce your rabbit your dog. The first meeting should be organized and planned in advance as many long-term problems occur if the first meeting is haphazard or poorly implemented. The point of the introduction process is for both animals to learn that being near to each other is rewarding, and for your dog to learn that chase is not an option. Therefore, ensure that you have nice treats for both the dog and the rabbit, as well as an indoor cage for your rabbit, and hold your dog loosely on his/her lead.

Try to avoid tightening the lead as this may cause your dog to lunge and pull away from the pressure and towards the rabbit. The aim is for your dog to settle down by the side of your rabbit's indoor cage with a chew whilst your rabbit eats some greens or hay. If your dog will not settle, repeat your 'leave' command along with a treat each time his attention leaves the rabbit. Try not to calm, reassure, control or reprimand your dog as all that attention is likely to make his or her behaviour worse.

Introduce your dog and rabbit gradually with short daily sessions but always try to finish on a high note – this way, you will all feel like repeating the exercise.

The next stage is to let the rabbit out of the cage with the dog still held on a loose lead. As rabbits don't tend to run around for long periods, the dog should soon lose interest, but the command 'leave' can be used if the dog gets too excited. When your rabbit ignores the rabbit, give a very exciting reward to ensure that he will keep responding to your commands.

A muzzle can be used at any stage if you are too nervous to hold the lead loosely or are unsure of your dog's response. Remember that your dog may not be able to take a treat with a muzzle on, and this will slow the progress of your training.

03 finding a rabbit

In this chapter you will learn:

- **about different rabbit breeds**
- **how to obtain a rabbit**
- **how to sex a young rabbit.**

The importance of early experience

Experiences during a sensitive period of behavioural development have a profound and lasting effect on an animal's behaviour. As young animals develop, everything that they encounter is considered 'normal'. In the wild this will be the family group, the surrounding habitat and environmental stimuli. Any experiences encountered at a later date will be classed as 'abnormal' and the animal will be fearful of them. This learning is necessary for animals to learn what to like and what to fear – for the rabbit, this teaches them to avoid predators but to accept members of their own group.

For positive associations to be formed during this sensitive period it is necessary for domestic rabbits to experience the types of stimuli they will live with in later life and it is this that makes the environment they are raised in so important.

As a general rule, the more exposure an animal has to humans, other animals, normal household noises and environmental stimuli when young, the better their behaviour will be when they are older. If a breeder starts to handle when the rabbit is young, research and experience have shown that this is likely to lead to bolder and less fearful adult rabbits.

In practice this means that if a breeder regularly handles rabbit kittens, starting when they areno older than three weeks, and then the new owners continue handling, these rabbits are less likely to display fearful behaviours towards their owner as an adult. It is worth noting that fear can be expressed as aggression so spending some time choosing the right breeder and investing some of your time with your rabbit when it is young has a significant pay-off later on.

Finding a rabbit

There are three main avenues for finding a rabbit – a breeder, a rescue centre or a pet shop.

Rabbit breeders fall into two categories: one-off or accidental breeders and 'professional' breeders. Accidental breeders tend to keep pet rabbits and, due to an accident (such as an escapee or mis-sexing rabbits) have had one litter and are looking for homes for the offspring. These rabbits are likely to be crossbreeds and can make good pets as they should be used to people, other pets and noises. These breeders are few and far between but are likely to advertise their rabbits on the local vet's notice board, in the local paper or in the pet shop window.

Professional breeders will sell a particular breed that they probably show. They are likely to be a member of the British Rabbit Council (see 'Taking it further' section at the end of this book for contact details) and may keep anything up to fifty or a hundred rabbits. If you are interested in a particular breed then there is a really good chance that you will get a very nice rabbit as well as lots of really helpful information as rabbit breeders tend to know an awful lot about rabbits.

It is worth bearing in mind that show rabbits can be bred for their looks rather than temperament and it is hard to regularly handle fifty plus rabbits which means that the rabbits might have a tendency towards nervous behaviour around unusual people. My advice is to speak to several breeders, only buy from a breeder that is happy for you to visit them, be prepared to travel and wait for a litter from the breeder that you like the sound of.

There are some rabbit breeders who are not interested in showing their animals and are simply providing the pet trade. They often produce rabbits in large numbers with little interest in the individual health or welfare of the animals. This practice has parallels with a puppy farm and raises the same concerns.

Rescue centres are often full of rabbits and many of them are there because somebody lost interest in them or didn't understand them enough to look after them properly. There is a general feeling that taking on a rescue animal means that you are taking on 'somebody else's problems' but being able to give a home to a rescue animal is really rewarding (plus the information in this book will help!). Asking for as much history as possible, including how the rabbit has been behaving towards people, can help you to make the right decision. If you are hoping to mix a rescue rabbit with your existing rabbit then ask if the rabbit has interacted with other rabbits in the shelter.

Rabbits make wonderful pets at any age. In some ways, 'veteran' rabbits are slightly easier to own as they toilet train easily and are unlikely to suddenly develop a behaviour problem so should not be discounted during a visit to a rescue centre.

Pet shops are either very good or very bad. A really good pet shop will have staff that are really passionate about rabbits, will spend time with you before you make your decision, will show you how to handle your rabbit(s) and will send you home with care leaflets, the correct food and hutch. A poor pet shop may be selling very young rabbits that are not very healthy, will give you little advice and will only seem interested in the sale. Don't buy a rabbit from here just because you wonder what will happen to it them you don't – the more we purchase from these establishments, the more rabbits they will buy in, and so the cycle continues.

Choosing a breed

There are over 65 breeds of rabbit recognized by the British Rabbit Council, over 45 in the United States and well over 100 rabbit breeds worldwide. When rabbits are exhibited, the breeds are classified into Fancy, Lops, Fur and Rex rabbits (see Chapter 09). Listed below is a short profile of the most common breeds in alphabetic order followed by a general description of the main colours (please note, exact colour descriptions vary between breeds. For further information contact the British Rabbit Council or the American Rabbit Breeders Association (ARBA), details in the 'Taking it further' section at the end of this book).

Angora (English)

Description:

Originally the Angora was called the 'White Shock Turkey Rabbit' and is considered to be one of the oldest known breeds of domestic rabbits. In the 1700s it was exported to France and was crossed with other breeds to create coloured varieties.

The Angora rabbit produces Angora fur, but this is often confused with the Angora goat that actually produces mohair. The fibre is hollow and is said to be three times warmer than lamb's wool.

The Angora is round and snowball-like and weighs around 3.4kg (7.5lbs). The fur is silky and covers the whole body, including the feet with tufts on the tips of the ears. Its head is broad and short with dense fur.

Suitability as pet:

Although the Angora is a very attractive animal, its fur requires daily grooming and would make this breed unsuitable as a pet for anyone other than an experienced owner.

Recognized colours:

White or Coloured (Golden, Sooty Fawn, Cream, Blue-cream, Sable, Chocolate, Smoke, Blue, Brown-Grey, Blue-Grey, Chinchilla and Cinnamon).

Belgian Hare

Description:

The Belgian Hare was introduced into the UK from Belgium in 1874 before being exported to America in the late nineteenth century. It has been used for meat production, particularly during the Second World War and is now a popular show animal.

Many people can be fooled into believing that this is a hare rather than a rabbit, such is the similarity. In appearance, the Belgian hare is graceful with a long muscular flank, an arched back with rounded hindquarters and large ears. The front legs are long and fine and the back legs are flat. The Belgian hare comes in just one colour, a rich chestnut colour with some black markings on the body, but not the chest or face.

Suitability as a pet:

The Belgian hare can make a good pet if it is handled well, offered companionship and provided with sufficient space to have regular exercise.

Beveren

Description:

Beverens originated in a town called Beveren in Belgium and were one of the most popular breeds of rabbit to be bred for their fur whilst also making a good meat breed. Their original coat colour is lavender blue. They have dense, silky hair that is between 25 and 30mm long and weigh approximately 3.62kg (8lbs). Beverens have a long back and well-furred prominent ears. Their body shape, when sitting is said to mirror the curves of a mandolin.

Suitability as pet:

Beverens are quite large rabbits and usually have a good temperament.

Recognized colours:

Blue, White, Black, Brown and Lilac.

British Giant

Description:

The media's favourite rabbit was first bred in the 1940s and exhibited in the 1960s. As the name suggests, British Giant rabbits are the largest rabbits weighing at least 5.6kg (12.4lbs) with a long and flat muscular body. They also have very large stand-up ears which can reach 19 cm (7.5 inches) in length.

Suitability as a pet:

The British Giant's size means that it can make a good indoor pet but will require confident handling and may not live as long as a smaller breed. It will require deep bedding to prevent sore hocks.

Recognized colours:

White, Black, Dark Steel Grey, Blue, Brown Grey and Opal.

figure 3 British Giant with Polish rabbit

Californian

Description:

The Californian is an American breed, produced by breeding Himalayan/Chinchilla crosses with New Zealand whites. The early rabbits were very good meat, and fur rabbits were shown for the first time towards the end of the 1920s.

The Californian is a medium-sized rabbit weighing around 4.3kg (9.5lb) with well-developed shoulders, a broad head, short neck and legs and a straight tail. The coat lies smooth and when brushed against itself returns to its original position. The rabbit has shorter fur on its stomach and its nose, ears, feet and tail are coloured with strong points whilst the body is pure white.

Suitability as pet:

The Californian can make a good pet if it is handled well, offered companionship and provided with sufficient space to have regular exercise.

Recognized colours:

Chocolate, Lilac and Blue points.

Cashmere Lop

Description:

The Cashmere Lop originates from the Dwarf Lop and was recognized as a breed in the UK during the 1990s. Cashmere Lops are standard size (2.15kg or 4.74lbs) or mini (1.6kg or 3.5lbs) and both are recognized by the British Rabbit Council.

Cashmere Lops have a silky coat which should not be matted. Their ears are lop and described as horseshoe-shaped. Overall the body looks compact and muscled.

Suitability as a pet:

As the Cashmere Lop requires daily grooming it is not recommended as a pet.

Recognized colours:

White, Black, Brown, Blue-eyed White, Agouti pattern (Agouti, Chinchilla, Opal, Squirrel), Shaded (Siamese Sable, Siamese

Smoke, Sealpoint, Sooty Fawn, Beige, Iron Grey, Bluepoint), Tan Pattern (Fox, Marten Sable, Marten Smoke, Otter) and other colours (Fawn, Orange, Steel and Butterfly pattern).

Chinchilla

Description:

The Chinchilla is a very attractive rabbit with a slate blue-grey, soft, silky coat that closely resembles the better-known chinchilla animal, *Chinchilla lanigera*, which originates from Chile and Peru. The name Chinchilla describes the rabbit's fur, which is very dense and soft. Consequently this rabbit was originally bred for its fur, which was highly sought after.

An adult Chinchilla weighs 3.06kg (6.75lbs) and it is quite acceptable for females to develop a slight dewlap of skin under the chin. The Chinchilla Giganta is a larger version of the standard Chinchilla rabbit weighing 5.44kg (12lbs).

Suitability as a pet:

Both the Chinchilla and the Chinchilla Giganta can make good pets if they are handled well, offered companionship and provided with sufficient space to have regular exercise. Their coats require regular grooming.

Dutch

Description:

Dutch rabbits, along with the English, were the most popular pet and exhibition rabbits – a position that has now been filled by the Lop breeds. Originally from Holland or Belgium, the breed is striking in its appearance with a white blaze carrying up to a point between the ears, a saddle of colour continuing right around the middle of the rabbit with a straight edge and white markings on the hind feet. Their coat should be glossy and they are a medium-sized rabbit weighing approx. 2.26kg (4.85lbs).

Suitability as a pet:

Dutch rabbits are very lively and alert and can make fun pets, although a prospective owner should be looking for a breeder that handles the rabbits regularly from a young age, ensuring that the rabbit is not too sensitive.

Recognized colours:

Black, Blue, Chocolate, Yellow, Tortoiseshell, Steel Grey, Brown Grey and Pale Grey on a white body.

Dwarf Lop

Description:

The Dwarf Lop is a very popular pet and exhibition rabbit. Produced from the French Lop, the Dwarf Lop first appeared in Holland in the 1950s and is known as the Holland Lop in America. The breed was recognized by the British Rabbit Council in 1976. Dwarf Lops have a 'cobby' well-muscled appearance and weigh approx. 2kg (4lbs 4oz). They have broad lop ears that are carried close to the head to give a horseshoe-like appearance. Their coat is dense and quite long.

Suitability as a pet:

Dwarf Lops are thought to be placid rabbits, so can make a good pet if handled well, offered companionship and provided with sufficient space to have regular exercise.

Recognized colours:

White, Black, Blue, Brown, Agouti Pattern (Agouti, Chinchilla, Opal), Shaded (Siamese Sable, Light, Dark, Siamese Smoke, Sealpoint, Sooty Fawn), Tan Pattern (Black Fox, Blue Fox, Chocolate Fox, Lilac Fox, Sable Marten Dark, Marten Medium and Light), Fawn, Orange, Steel, Butterfly.

English

Description:

The English rabbit, also known as the English Spot, is a very well known breed and a common pet, having been in existence within the UK for over 200 years.

An English rabbit weighs between 2.7 to 3.6 kgs (5.9 to 7.9lbs). Its markings are very distinctive with a white body and coloured spots, coloured ears, coloured smut on the nose and an unbroken coloured line along the spine. Ideally the markings on both sides should be equally balanced and the spots should increase in size towards the rump.

Suitability as a pet:

The English rabbit is a medium-sized rabbit with very few specialized requirements. As long as it has been handled regularly from a young age and is gradually introduced into a new home it is likely to make a very good pet.

Recognized colours:

The colours for the spots and markings can be Black, Blue, Tortoiseshell, Chocolate or Grey.

English Lop

Description:

The first of the Lop rabbits, the English Lop was the first rabbit to be bred purely for exhibition (as opposed to meat or fur) leading to the title 'King of the Fancy' which still exists today. The English Lop remains an exhibition breed and is not a very common pet rabbit. Crosses with continental giant breeds led to the development of the French Lop, and from the French came other breeds such as the Dwarf Lop.

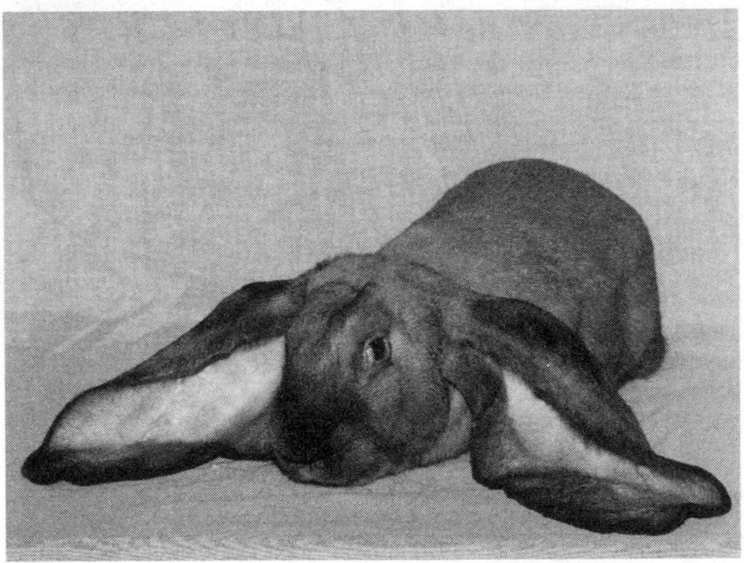

figure 4 English Lop

The English Lop is very distinctive with incredibly long lop ears, a bold head and large body size. The rabbit can weigh around 5.5kg (12.10lbs).

On 1 November 2003 the ears of an English Lop called Nipper's Geronimo were measured at 79cm (31.1inches) in a complete span at the ARBA National Show in Wichita, Kansas, USA. They are recorded as a Guinness World Record.

Suitability as a pet:

The English Lop needs an experienced owner and lots of space. They are often quite placid and friendly animals but could become fearful if handled badly. They require a large living area to prevent them from damaging their ears.

Recognized colours:

Black, Fawn, White, Golden Fawn, Sooty Fawn or Marked.

Flemish Giant

Description:

These rabbits, as the name suggests, originated from Belgium and are thought to have been developed as early as the nineteenth century. The British variety was developed during the early 1920s and is only recognized in one colour, Steel Grey.

The Flemish Giant is a large rabbit weighing around 4.9kg (10.8lbs), although it is normal for females to weigh up to 5.44kg (11.9lbs) and to have a slight dewlap of skin under the chin. Their stomachs and feet are white and the body shape is wide and flatter than the British Giant.

Suitability as a pet:

The Flemish Giant's size means that it can make a good indoor pet but will require confident handling and may not live as long as a smaller breed. It will require deep bedding to prevent sore hocks.

French Lop

Description:

This breed originates from France and was created during the middle of the nineteenth century. It was introduced into the UK primarily as a meat rabbit but in 1965, the French Lop was exhibited for the first time – to this day, they remain a very popular exhibition and pet rabbit.

The French Lop is a large rabbit, weighing more than 4.5kg (9.9lbs). It has lop ears and an almost cubic appearance, with a short thickset body and large head.

Suitability as a pet:

As a large rabbit, the French Lop can be quite placid but is as likely to develop behaviour problems as other breeds. Their size dictates confident handling and they will require a large hutch/run to move around freely. They are not the rabbit for small children or people who have limited space, although they can live in the house as a house pet.

Recognized colours:

Black, White, Brown, Blue, Agouti, Chinchilla, Opal, Sooty Fawn, Siamese Sable, Orange, Fawn, Steel and Butterfly.

Himalayan

Description:

The Himalayan has had many names including the Black Nosed Rabbit, Warren Rabbit and the Egyptian Smut, but it is not thought to have originated in the area of the Himalayan Mountains. The fur of Himalayan rabbits was once highly sought after across the world but the rabbit is now a popular show rabbit.

The Himalayan is a white rabbit with a darker smut on the nose matching the colour of the ears and the legs. It weighs approx. 2kg (4.41lbs) and is born with no colour markings – these are caused by temperature differences and develop when the rabbit leaves the nest.

Suitability as a pet:

The Himalayan is considered to have a very docile nature. In the right situation, they can make a really good pet.

Recognized colours:

The marking colour includes black, blue and chocolate.

Lionhead

Description:

The exact origins of the Lionhead are unclear but it is thought that the lion-like ruff around the head is a genetic mutation and this can be traced back to Belgium. The Lionhead is a relatively new breed to the UK and has become a common pet due to its attractive appearance and small size.

Lionhead rabbits weigh approx. 1.7kg (3.7lbs) with small erect ears and a compact body. The mane of hair is 5–7.5cms (2–3 inches) long and extends around the head with longer hair on the chest and cheeks. They can occur in a variety of common colours.

Suitability as a pet:

As with all long-haired breeds, the Lionhead requires regular grooming but its small size also suggests that it requires an experienced owner who is confident in handling.

Miniature Lion Lop

Description:

One of the newest breeds of rabbit, the Miniature Lion Lop was recognized by the British Rabbit Council in 2004. The breed is similar in size and shape to the Miniature Lop, but with the addition of a mane, similar to the Lionhead. The Miniature Lion Lop came into the UK as quite a large rabbit and was then bred to improve the size and appearance. The UK was the first country worldwide to accept this new breed.

Suitability as a pet:

As with all long-haired breeds, the Lion Lop requires regular grooming, but its small size also suggests that it requires an experienced owner who is confident in handling.

Recognized colours:

Black, Blue, Agouti, Sooty Fawn, Fawn, Black Fox, Black Otter.

Miniature Lop

Description:

Miniature Lops were recognized by the British Rabbit Council in 1994 having been developed from the Dwarf Lop (miniature) introduced from Holland.

The Miniature Lop is a thickset and firm rabbit weighing just 1.5kg (3.3lbs). The ears are lopped but thick and broad, hanging to give a horseshoe outline to the head. The coat is dense and the front legs are thick, short and straight. They can be any recognized colour pattern.

Suitability as a pet:

Miniature Lops are very popular pets and are considered to have a good temperament, however they are a small rabbit and require careful and confident handling.

Netherland Dwarf

Description:

The Netherland Dwarf is a very well known pet and exhibition rabbit. Introduced into the UK in 1950, the Netherland Dwarf was originally developed in Holland from the Polish rabbit. Initially the breed suffered with inherited tooth and eye problems, but responsible breeding seems to have overcome this problem.

The Netherland Dwarf is a very small rabbit, weighing no more than 1.1kg (2.4lbs). Its appearance is compact with a full chest, wide shoulders, round head and eyes with erect ears.

Suitability as a pet:

Their cute appearance and size appeals to many pet owners but as a small rabbit the Netherland Dwarf requires regular handling when young to avoid problems associated with nervousness (including aggression). Owners should be experienced, so they are perhaps not the best breed for young children.

Recognized colours:

White, Black, Blue, Brown, Lilac, Shaded (Sable, Smoke Pearl, Seal Point, Tortoiseshell), Agouti (Agouti, Opal, Lynx, Chinchilla, Squirrel), Tan (Tan, Foxes, Sable Marten, Otter), Orange, Fawn, Steel, Himalayan.

New Zealand

Description:

The New Zealand rabbit is a large rabbit routinely used as a meat and laboratory rabbit but also a popular pet and exhibition rabbit. New Zealand rabbits originate from America, not New Zealand. The New Zealand White first appeared in 1917 in America and was imported into the UK after the Second World War (1945).

The New Zealand rabbit grows very quickly, perhaps one of the reasons for its popularity as a meat rabbit. An adult rabbit can weigh up to 5.44kg (12lb) with a medium body, well-rounded haunches, short front legs and a bold head. The coat is usually dense but soft. The New Zealand Red is a different, smaller rabbit than the New Zealand White, typically weighing 3.62kg (8lbs).

Suitability as a pet:

As a large rabbit, the New Zealand may be less prone to nervousness. However, its weight might be off-putting for people that wish to handle the breed regularly.

Recognized colours:

White, Black, Blue.

Polish

Description:

Polish rabbits are the smallest recognized breed of rabbit, weighing just 0.9kg (2lb). Originally bred as a luxury meat, they originated in the UK rather than Poland and were exported to America in 1912 where they have been bred as a larger variety. In Scandinavia and Holland, the Polish rabbit is called the Dwarf Hare for its sprightly nature and appearance. The Polish has a short, close fur and small erect ears.

Suitability as a pet:

Polish are not recommended as pets due to their small size and need very specialized handling.

Recognized colours:

White, Black, Blue, Brown, Lilac, Shaded Self (Sable, Smoke Pearl, Agouti, Opal, Lynx, Squirrel, Chinchilla), Tan Patterned (Tan, Fox, Sable Marten, Smoke Pearl Marten), other varieties (Orange, Fawn, Tortoiseshell, Steel), marked (Himalayan).

Rex

Description:

Rex rabbits have a particular type of fur that resembles velvet. This is caused by reduced guard hairs, which are the long and strong hairs in a rabbit coat. This quality made their fur the most valuable in the fur trade at one time.

An adult Rex is approximately 3kg (6.6lbs) in weight whilst a Mini Rex, the newest addition, may weigh up to 1.8kg (3.9lbs). Their shape is close to that of the wild rabbit with erect ears, a bold head, strong hind legs and a graceful posture.

Suitability as a pet:

Although Rex can sometime have sensitive temperaments, they are very appealing rabbits that are a good size for a pet.

Recognized colours:

Ermine, Black, Blue, Havana, Shaded (Smoke Pearl Siamese, Smoke Pearl Marten, Siamese Seal, Siamese Sable, Tortoiseshell), Tan (Marten Sable, Marten Seal, Orange, Fawn, Otter Rex), Agouti (Castor, Chinchilla, Opal, Lynx, Cinnamon), Dalmatian, Harlequin, Himalayan, Silver Seal and Satin.

Silver Fox

Description:

The first Silver Fox rabbits were exhibited in 1926, having been created from the original Chinchilla breed. In America, the Silver Fox is called the Silver Marten with their own Silver Fox a much larger rabbit, created by crossing Checkered Giants with Silvers.

The Silver Fox rabbit has a coat of even colour with white ticking from silver-tipped hairs around the chest, flanks and feet. The rabbit has brown, grey or lilac eyes and each eye is circled neatly with an under colour. The coat is very dense but beautifully silky. An adult Silver Fox can weigh up to 3.17kg (7lb).

Suitability as a pet:

The Silver Fox can make a good pet if it is handled well, offered companionship and provided with sufficient space to have regular exercise.

Recognized colours:

Black (dark blue under colour), Blue, Chocolate (slate under colour), Lilac.

Tan

Description:

Tans are one of the oldest breeds of rabbit having been first found in Britain during the 1880s. The Tan is thought to have been created by mixing some Dutch and crossbreed rabbits with wild rabbits and is now a very popular show rabbit.

In appearance, the Tan has a coloured back and a light coloured (tan) belly and flanks that may come up to cover the ears, nostrils and feet.

It is a compact and very attractive rabbit and an adult can weigh 1.9kg (4.1lbs).

Suitability as a pet:

The Tan can make a good pet if it is handled well, offered companionship and provided with sufficient space to have regular exercise.

Recognized colours:

Blue and Tan, Chocolate and Tan, Lilac and Tan.

Rabbit colours and markings

Some of the colours and markings recognized by the British Rabbit Council are self-explanatory but some require a brief description.

Agouti – refers to two colours on the same strand of hair. The normal agouti is the grey-brown colour of the wild rabbit.

Blue – an even blue-grey colour.

Broken marked – similar to the butterfly but with varied markings on an otherwise white fur.

Butterfly – white on underbelly, chest, feet and nose, leaving a colour on the back, ears and a distinctive butterfly marking on the head.

Chinchilla – refers to the dark silver-grey colour of the animal with the same name. The hair has three tones with the under colour dark blue, the middle colour white and the tips black.

Chocolate – an even dark-brown colour.

Cinnamon – the hair is an agouti hair with a bright golden tan at the top and a light orange on a blue under colour.

Dalmatian – a white rabbit with small coloured patches that may be a single colour or bi-coloured.

Fox – most of the hair shaft is the body colour, which is usually black, blue, lilac or chocolate. The chest, side and feet of the rabbit should be 'ticked' with white hairs and the eye circles, inside of ears, underside of tail and belly are white.

Harlequin – the coat is a mix of two colours, usually black and bright orange.

Havana – an even, dark-chocolate colour.

Lilac – a dove-grey colour.

Lynx – each hair has a top colour of orange-silver, intermediate colour of bright orange and a white under colour.

Opal – each hair has a top band of blue, intermediate colour of gold and a slate blue under colour.

Otter – a black, blue, chocolate or lilac coloured rabbit with a pale beige stomach.

Sable – a rich sepia colour on the face and body leading to a paler colour on the sides and stomach.

Sable Marten – body colour as for sable but with white hairs giving a 'ticking' effect to the chest, sides, rump and feet.

Sealpoint – a beige-grey body with a darker grey face, ears, legs, feet and tail.

Siamese Sable – similar to Sealpoint but the body is brown whilst the sides, face, ears, legs, feet and tail are dark grey.

Siamese Smoke – similar to Sealpoint but the body is blue-grey whilst the sides, face, ears, legs, feet and tail are dark grey.

Silver – white hairs ('ticking') spread evenly all over the coat, which is usually black.

Smoke Pearl – the body and head are a smoky grey colour that becomes a grey-beige on the sides, chest and stomach.

Sooty Fawn – an orange-brown top coat with blue under colour.

Squirrel – a blend of blue and white so that each hair has an under colour of slate blue with an intermediate white band and blue tops.

Steel – a dark version of the agouti.

Tortoiseshell – similar to the Sooty Fawn.

Choosing a rabbit

The decision as to which rabbit you pick from a litter is often dictated by the sex that you would prefer. After that it invariably goes on looks, particularly with the marked breeds that may differ in appearance.

An initial health check should ensure that the young rabbit's eyes are bright and not runny, breathing is easy and there do not appear to be any nasal blockages. The area around the anus – under the tail – should be clean and not stained. Whilst it is not easy to determine an ideal weight, the ribs of the baby should not be jutting out and there should be a good covering of flesh over the neck and body.

As a person approaches the hutch you should feel that the mother and her babies are interested in their presence but are not overly excitable. The kittens should be watched whilst they move about to ensure that they move easily and that there is no aggression between individuals.

Before interacting with your chosen rabbit, it helps to roll your hands in some dirty bedding so that your smell does not cause any problems. Make sure that the young rabbit does not seem to be scared or particularly jumpy as this may lead to a nervous adult that could be difficult to handle. Ask to be shown how to correctly handle the rabbit and check that he or she seems to be relaxed whilst this is being done.

Male or female?

If you have decided to have one rabbit, you may be unsure which sex to have. If you are having two young kittens it is very important for them to be sexed correctly to prevent problems later on.

There is a skill involved in sexing rabbits – even some experts make mistakes! There are very few obvious external differences between males and females so they can only be sexed once they are on their backs. Their sexual organs are located on their lower abdomen at the base of the tail.

In mature rabbits the males are obviously different to the females by the scrotal sacs that should be visible inside both of the hind legs. Young rabbits can be sexed with the middle finger holding down the tail and the thumb pressed at the top of the genital opening. This method causes the penis of the male to protrude; no protrusion would suggest a female.

sexing a young
buck rabbit
up to four months

sexing a
doe rabbit

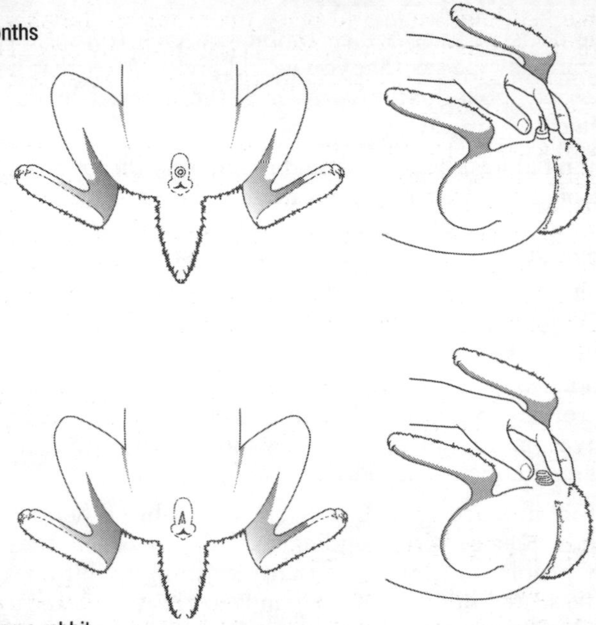

figure 5 sexing a rabbit

Behaviourally there is a slight difference between the sexes and this can affect their ability to make good pets. In general, males tend to be a bit easier although they can be more territorial than females – sometimes spraying urine around the territory, or displaying sexual behaviour once they reach maturity (between four and six months depending on the breed). Females, on the other hand, can become quite aggressive when they reach maturity particularly during the spring months. They too can spray urine onto the hutch, around the home or onto their owners. Often these behaviours, in both sexes, calm down with age or neutering.

Bringing your rabbit home

Before you buy your rabbit, make sure that you already have the hutch, plenty of bedding, food bowls, a hayrack, some toys, a water bottle, some hay and food. It is not advisable to purchase all these items once you have the rabbit in the car as a prolonged time in the car can greatly increase the rabbit's feelings of stress.

Take a sturdy cardboard box or travelling cage with a towel or some bedding inside and place the rabbit in the passenger foot well or on the back seat with a belt around the box. Try to leave the rabbit alone during the journey and make sure that the car is well ventilated.

The digestive system of the rabbit is very sensitive and can easily be affected by stress – such as a change of environment or the introduction of a new food. When this happens, the rabbit may become bloated and constipated and can become quite sick. It is really important to introduce the rabbit to its new home and then leave it alone with some of the food that it was eating in its previous home. If you are not offered this food by the seller – ask!

A new food can be introduced after several days by mixing the two diets together and then gradually reducing the amount of the original feed.

The first few days

Your new rabbit needs time to accustom itself to you, your home and its new house. For the first few days, your rabbit should be interacted with gently but regularly (particularly if you suspect that it is scared of you). Gentle stroking can be introduced when he or she is eating and just sitting and watching will tell you a lot about your rabbit and enable them to get used to your presence.

If your rabbit is going to live in the house, make sure that the indoor cage has been placed in a quiet room of the home. Placing the rabbit's cage in a hallway, for example, will not make them feel very secure and could lead to the development of problems in the future. Keeping the rabbit in the cage for a few days will help them to learn that this is their space and will give them a chance to accustom themselves to the sounds and smells of your home.

Keeping them in the cage initially also helps with toilet training as the rabbit should select a corner as their latrine within a couple of days. Once this has happened the litter tray can be placed in that location with some of the dirty bedding inside to encourage the rabbit to return. If you continue to have problems with toilet training you might find that these improve with neutering.

If you have obtained your new rabbit as a companion for another, start the introduction process after the rabbit has been with you for about a week. If you need to have either rabbit neutered, do this before you start the introduction and wait four weeks after the operation to ensure that any stored sperm have gone and that stitches cannot be pulled out.

04 nutrition

In this chapter you will learn:

- **about fibre**
- **how to feed your rabbit**
- **what to do if your rabbit is overweight.**

In this section we will discuss the best way to feed your rabbit to ensure that they stay healthy and happy. We know that diets that are high in sugar, fat or processed foods are not good for us and they are less good for the rabbit that evolved to eat high quantities of a low-quality food, such as grass.

There are many different rabbit feeds available and it is easy to be persuaded by price or packaging but confused by the benefits. Listed below are the main ingredients of a healthy diet – fibre, green leaves, pellets/mix and treats.

Fibre

Rabbits need to eat high quantities of fibre to stay healthy but what is fibre and how can you spot it? Plant fibre is also known as cellulose and is found in vegetation. Suitable high-fibre foods for rabbits include hay, alfalfa, grass and leafy green vegetables.

Without fibre the sensitive digestive system of the rabbit can fail, as it requires an even supply of long-strand fibre to ensure constant gut movement – if this is affected, problems such as constipation, bloat or diarrhoea can develop.

Feeding a diet high in fibre increases the amount of time that your rabbit spends eating. We know that the wild rabbit can spend up to 70 per cent of its time outside the burrow grazing – this means approximately four or five hours every day. Most commercial rabbit foods take the rabbit a short amount of time to eat leaving them with lots of spare time but, perhaps most importantly, their teeth may not be worn down effectively. When a rabbit eats hay it takes several seconds for them to eat each strand, and whilst this is happening the teeth are rubbing together equally. As a rabbit's teeth grow continuously throughout their life it is important that they are worn down by the continual action of tearing and grinding.

Increasing the amount of time that a rabbit spends eating in addition to feeding a fibrous diet can help to reduce or prevent behavioural problems. Rabbits that are destructive or overgroom themselves (or another rabbit) may be responding to a lack of fibre in their diet. Rabbits in pain from dental disease or digestive disturbances can become withdrawn or aggressive. Bored rabbits are also likely to be more destructive, particularly in the home where hay is usually not offered as it is considered too messy.

Alfalfa, which provides a very good source of fibre and protein, also contains compounds called oxalates and high calcium levels that can cause kidney problems in some individuals.

A diet that is high in fibre can prevent a rabbit developing digestive problems, dental disease, behavioural problems, bladder stones, obesity and fly strike.

Fibre should make up the majority of the rabbit's diet each day and it should have *continual* access to good quality hay or grass. Hay can be stuffed into a hayrack to keep it clean but must be kept permanently topped up.

There are several types of hay or grass available:

Timothy hay – this type of grass seed hay is considered to be very good for rabbits due to the high ratio of stem to leaf which leads to high levels of fibre, particularly in the first cut of the growing season. Timothy hay is not commonly grown in the UK so may be imported from America and Canada.

Barn dried hay – the hay is dried using forced draught-ventilation which helps to remove moulds and spores. The resulting grass hay is easy for animals to digest and has retained most of its nutrients. Some producers medicate the hay to remove any bacteria.

Meadow hay – contains a variety of grasses and may contain dried flowers and seed heads. It is quite easy for rabbits to digest but must be free from mould, be slightly green and should have a sweet odour.

Alfalfa hay – alfalfa is a legume hay, resembling clover with clusters of small purple flowers. It contains higher levels of protein and calcium than other types of hay whilst still providing a high fibre diet.

Grasses – dried grass can contain high levels of fibre and minerals and is often cut short which makes it less messy to feed. Fresh grass from the garden is acceptable in small amounts but must not be fed if there is a risk of contamination with fertilizers or animal urine nor if it has been cut using a lawnmower due to the effect of fuel fumes and rapid fermentation. You can make your own hay by cutting grass and nettles early in the summer and drying them (without heating) by hanging them or spreading out on wire racks and turning regularly.

Always ensure that hay or dried grass is stored in an area that is dry and well-ventilated to prevent mould.

Green leaves

Green vegetables (such as cabbage, broccoli, greens, kale, carrot tops), herbs (such as basil and parsley), as well as plant matter (such as dandelion, plantain and blackberry leaves) can add some variety and fibre to the rabbit's diet. They should be introduced gradually, particularly to young rabbits, and always washed first (there is a list of dangerous plants in Chapter 10).

Contrary to folklore, rabbits should not eat some types of lettuce (such as iceberg) as they contain a substance called laudanum which can be harmful in large quantities. Similarly, carrots and apples are not recommended for regular consumption due to their high natural sugar content.

figure 6 green vegetables and leaves are an essential part of a rabbit's high-fibre diet

Pellets and mixes

Pellets and mixes should be seen as a complimentary food alongside hay and green vegetable matter.

Extruded pellets contain all the nutrients, fibre and minerals that the rabbit requires and can be considered a complete food. The extrusion process makes the pellets more palatable and easier to digest.

Rabbit mixes are quite colourful and contain a variety of ingredients including dried peas, maize, oats, barley and grass pellets. Some mixes have added molasses that makes them sticky and some have hay included into the mix. Although the mix is intended to provide a complete meal, rabbits tend to pick out the best bits and leave the bits that they don't like. If the owner removes the rabbit's leftovers and replenishes the bowl the rabbit will keep eating only the best bits and will not be getting a complete diet. Only refill a bowl of rabbit mix when it is empty!

Pellets prevent rabbits from picking out the pieces of the food that they like and can stop selective feeding. However, they can sometimes contain too much protein and not enough fibre to be beneficial to the rabbit long term and do not provide sufficient dental wear on their own. Good pellets should contain at least 18 per cent fibre and less than 16 per cent protein.

Rabbits excrete the calcium that they do not need through their urine and absorb the rest. There are substances in grains and beans called phytic acid and oxalates in some plants (such as spinach) that prevent this absorption, leading to a build-up and the development of stones within the bladder. Grains and beans are present in many commercial rabbit mixes.

Pellets and mixes should be fed as a supplement to a hay or grass based diet – for a medium-sized rabbit (such as a Rex or English) this means just one handful a day.

Water

There must be a continual supply of fresh water either in a bottle or a bowl. The water should be changed daily and bottles cleaned regularly so that they are free of green algae.

Treats

We all like treats and we also like to spoil those that we care for, but many of the treats available for rabbits are full of sugar or fat – substances that the rabbit would never eat in the wild. Treats such as those made from hay, small pieces of vegetables (such as broccoli) or some herbs will be rewarding and healthy whilst carrots and fruit should be fed sparingly due to their high sugar content.

Additives

There are many additives available that are either included in the pellet or mix that we feed our rabbits or can be added afterwards. In general, if a rabbit is fed a simple diet (as outlined above) there should be no need to supplement the diet with any vitamins, minerals, additives or medications. However, older rabbits or those recuperating from an illness can benefit from a more specialized diet.

Common additives include the following:

- **Coccidiostat**: added to pellets (known as ACS pellets) to reduce levels of the parasite *Eimeria* which can cause Coccidiosis (see Chapter 10).
- **Antibiotics**: pellets with antibiotics added can only be obtained on prescription and may be used by breeders who have lost significant numbers of young rabbits at or after weaning to diarrhoea or bloating. In some circles it is considered that these health problems may arise as a consequence of poor feeding regimes and inter-breeding, as problems of this nature are rarely seen in the pet rabbit or in small studs of rabbits.
- **Extract of yucca**: is considered to reduce the odours from faeces or urine.
- **Echinacea**: is added to help the body's resistance to infections.
- **B vitamins**: are responsible for providing energy to the body during the conversion of glucose, from carbohydrates. They are also required for the metabolism of both fats and proteins, as well as the health and maintenance of the body's nervous system.
- **Vitamin E**: is an antioxidant and 'neutralises' free radicals within the body. This action helps to prevent cell damage and disease.

Probiotics and prebiotics

When a rabbit is born, its gastrointestinal tract is relatively sterile and the stomach pH is a neutral 5–6.5. By three weeks of age, however, the pH of the stomach has reduced to a more acidic 1–2 and bacteria are then able to move through and colonize the caecum (where the small intestine joins the colon).

In a healthy rabbit the amount of the bacteria *Clostridia* will be totally outnumbered by the microflora that is involved in the digestion process. Problems with the digestive systems of rabbits arise when the balance of bacteria within the caecum is altered and *Clostridia* are able to grow to unacceptable levels (this is known as dysbiosis).

This can happen when the rabbit is being fed the wrong diet, after a course of antibiotics or at stressful times such as weaning, travelling, mating, if overcrowded or living in poor conditions.

Mucoid enteritis is a condition seen in rabbits around the time of weaning that results from ileus (a lack of movement in the intestines) enabling *Clostridia* to multiply. The treatment of Mucoid enteritis is very difficult and there is little hope of success once the condition has been realized, but preventative measures include the use of prebiotics and probiotics during high-risk times.

Prebiotics supply an energy source for the beneficial bacteria and promote an intestinal environment that favours their development. Many rabbit feed companies include a prebiotic in their rabbit feeds. Prebiotics may be included as the simple sugars Fructo-oligosaccharides (FOS) or Mono-oligosaccharide (MOS). They produce an intestinal environment that favours the development of beneficial bacteria over harmful bacteria. These harmful, or pathogenic, bacteria must attach to the intestinal wall, to prevent themselves being swept out of the gut with the normal passage of food. Once attached, they may produce toxins, which go on to produce the symptoms of the disease in the animal. However, these bugs bind to oligosaccharide molecules, so if these are present in the diet the harmful bacteria will bind to them, instead of the gut wall, and be removed from the gut in the faeces.

Probiotics contain live bacteria that compete with harmful bacteria to promote a healthy population of normal gut flora. For many years, rabbit breeders have advocated the feeding of the caecal pellets of a healthy rabbit to an unwell individual –

this is the simplest and easiest probiotic, but not very helpful if all your animals are sick or you only have one rabbit.

Many rabbit feeds contain a probiotic under a brand name (such as AviPro) or as a water supplement. Probiotics can be helpful for a rabbit that has been suffering a digestive upset to restore balance to the system.

Caecotrophs

Apart from fibre, the other important factor in the digestive system of the rabbit is the consumption of the caecotrophs (the first set of faeces). These smelly, sticky faeces contain bacteria and vitamins and provide vital nutrients for a healthy gut. If a rabbit is not fed a diet high in fibre, it can become overweight and not able to reach around to eat these nutritious pellets. If a diet is high in protein but not high in fibre the rabbit might not eat these faeces and any time caecotrophs stick to the rabbit's bottom they become a target for flies and fly strike.

Overweight rabbits

It is very easy for rabbits to become overweight when we control the amount of food that they have and if we reduce their territory size so that they have very little opportunity for exercise. Also, obesity has consequences for rabbits as for humans and can reduce fertility and shorten lifespan. Rabbits usually get obese from eating too much of every food other than hay – no rabbit got fat on grass!

Removing any treats from the diet is a must as fatty, sugary, starchy treats will mess up the digestive system and provide 'empty' calories. It is worth remembering that apparently healthy treats such as carrot or apple might not help a rabbit to lose weight as they contain high levels of sugar.

There are reduced calorie extruded pellets available for pets that can be fed alongside lots of hay. These rabbits also need to be encouraged to exercise and should be put into a run on the lawn or brought into the home on a daily basis. A companion rabbit can get some overweight individuals moving.

Pregnant/lactating does

Feeding pregnant or lactating does should not require a change of the diet if the rabbit is being fed a high-fibre diet. The quantities, however, need to gradually increase in line with the pregnancy and any concentrated mix or pellet must contain at least 16 per cent protein. Supplementing the diet with alfalfa should provide sufficient calcium to prevent the lactating doe from developing osteoporosis.

Growing rabbits

As rabbits become less dependent on their mother's milk they will start to nibble at food so it is important to offer continual access to a good quality hay at this stage and ensure that they are not eating too much of the mother's high protein mix or pellet. Once they are weaned and starting to grow, both the youngsters and the mother can be fed a mix or pellet that contains at least 16 per cent protein as a supplement to the hay, along with small amounts of green vegetables and occasional alfalfa to help strong bones develop.

A word about packaging

Feed manufacturers often pack their products in colourful and eye-catching packaging. They do this to encourage people to pick up their brand and to attract new customers. In pet shops, we can often buy rabbit food that is sold in clear plastic bags, allowing us to see what we are buying. Although we prefer to see the product it is important to understand that in order to maintain the quality of the product and ensure its nutritional completeness, it is essential to exclude both air and light from the feed. Letting air near the food leads to oxidation, and could introduce fungal spores or other contaminants. Certain types of light also degrade the value of the vitamins. So, products pre-packed in non-transparent, thick plastic or aluminium packs, with no 'window' through which the product can be seen, mean that our rabbit should be gaining the same level of nutrients in the last scoop as they did with the first.

In this chapter you will learn:

- **about everything you need to keep a rabbit**
- **how to keep your rabbit dry in the wet weather**
- **how to litter train your rabbit.**

Before bringing your rabbit home you will need to obtain several items. The best place to purchase equipment or feed for a rabbit is through an independent retailer such as a local pet shop, garden centre, online retailer or hutch manufacturer. The large pet supermarkets allow you to buy many products under one roof but it is sensible to shop around before buying a hutch as it needs to last many years.

Hutch or indoor cage

Hutches come in a variety of shapes and sizes and the right hutch for you is the one that fits well into your garden, is well built and sturdy, and is likely to keep your rabbit protected from the elements. Buying a cheap hutch now may seem to be a sensible decision but it may represent a false economy if you need to replace it within a few years. A decent hutch should last the lifetime of the rabbit.

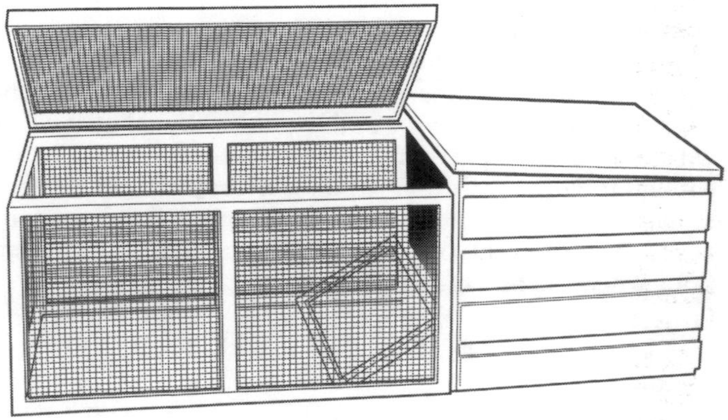

figure 7 hutch and run

The essentials of good rabbit housing are:

- **Space:** Many hutches seem to be made on a 'one size fits all' standard that does not allow the majority of rabbits enough room for movement. Whilst a rabbit can gain exercise roaming around the home or garden, its home should still offer room to move around, stretch out and hop backwards and forwards. The general rule is that the hutch should be high enough for an adult rabbit to stand upright on its back legs with enough length and width for it to be able to take several hops in any direction.
- **Quality:** Rabbits are quite robust and their hutches can have quite a hard time with chewing, digging and running around, so it is important that the hutch is made of a solid wood or plywood that feels sturdy when any pressure is put onto the joints. There should be no joins or edges that the rabbit can injure themselves on (or chew) and all nails should be embedded into the wood itself.
- **Durability:** The floors of the hutch should be at least 10mm (1/3 inch) thick and the doors should be heavy but not put too much strain on the hutch frame. The use of cheap plywood or thin flooring could lead to rotting or splitting within a few weeks of purchase.
- **Hygiene:** Without litter trays, one corner of the hutch will become sodden with dirty bedding so it is important for the hutch to have been treated with an animal-friendly varnish. The join between the floor and the sides should also be filled with a sealant to prevent seepage. Hutches should be open enough to allow the rabbit to have access to fresh air as well as natural light. Some hutches will come fitted with litter boards that prevent bedding falling out onto the garden or floor when the hutch door is opened.
- **Protection from the weather:** Hutches often come with one area enclosed as a sleeping area or with a panel that can be inserted into the door frame to keep the hutch (and its occupant) dry. Rabbits can usually cope well with a drop in temperature (assuming that they have sufficient bedding) but need protection from damp weather. However, this should not be at the expense of good ventilation so any covers or shutters should contain holes or slits that allow a flow of air through the hutch, and the hutch itself should stand at least 200–300mm (8–12 inches) off the floor with a gap of at least 250mm (10 inches)between the back of the hutch and any walls. This should help prevent respiratory problems in the

rabbit whilst allowing the hutch to dry. The roof of the hutch should have a thick mineralized felt attached and should slope backwards with a lip at the back to take any rain drips away from the back of the hutch.

- **Security**: Many a rabbit has been lost as a result of a badly built hutch or a faulty catch, so ensure that the hutch can withstand both the interest of a predator or your rabbit trying to escape. Metal button catches make effective latches along with small bolts at the base and top of doors. If you are concerned that predators, or even small children, might let the rabbit out, fit a padlock to the bolt. Two tiered hutches or hutches with runs in permanent place often allow the rabbit to be locked in at night (when predators are most likely to be around). The wire mesh in the doors or on the run should be thick and strong with no gaps. It should be stapled to the door at regular intervals; the gap between staples must be small enough to prevent a head or foot pushing through.

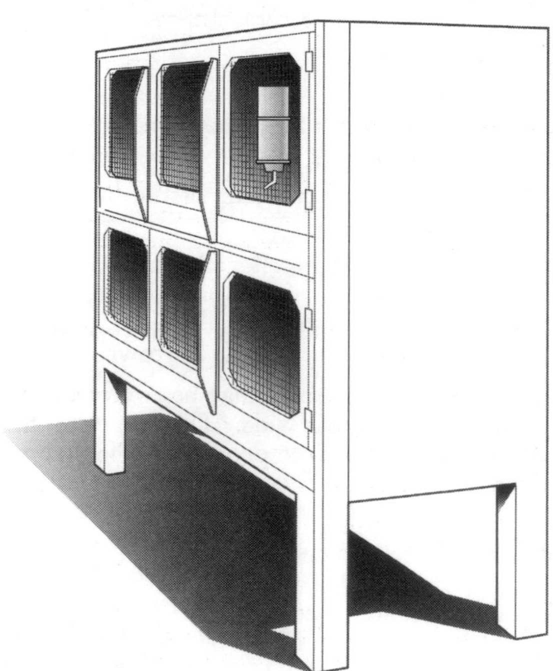

figure 8 block of hutches

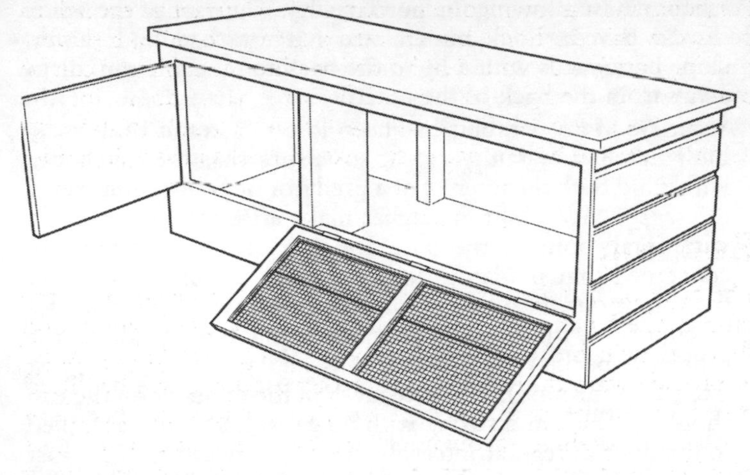

figure 9 one-storey hutch with enclosed nesting/sleeping area

Listed below is an overview of the most common hutch designs:

One storey – a traditional one storey hutch has a flat or gently sloped roof and may have one half of the hutch enclosed to provide a 'nesting area'.

Two storeys – a split-level hutch will include a ramp for the residents to move between levels. Some designs incorporate a run into the bottom level with a mesh base and sides to prevent the rabbit escaping down a self-made burrow!

Block hutch – a block of hutches may be two or three high and one or two compartments wide. This type of housing is commonly used by breeders or people with limited space and lots of rabbits.

Combined run and housing – these hutches are based on the design of early rabbit hutches and allow the rabbit to choose whether to stay outside or come into the sheltered hutch area. The rabbit can be secured into the hutch for safety reasons but the run should be sturdy enough to be predator proof.

Rabbit housing has traditionally been built from wood but there are now several moulded plastic homes that provide long-lasting and easy to clean environments.

For house rabbits, many outdoor hutches are attractive enough to be used within the home but an indoor cage (also called a puppy-training crate) makes an ideal home for a house rabbit and can be purchased in a variety of sizes. The same rules apply for the indoor cage as for the hutch – the rabbit must be able to stand on its back legs and have space to take several hops in any direction.

Bedding

The type of bedding used will depend on the location of the rabbit. The hutches of outdoor rabbits can be filled with wood shavings, which are highly absorbent, along with barley straw to provide warmth. Rabbits that are kept indoors will be 'litter' trained to toilet within a tray so this reduces the need for absorbent bedding throughout the cage and many owners provide their rabbits with a towel or square of veterinary bedding (called VetBed). Of course outdoors rabbits can still be litter trained so that their bedding, which will be different to the litter, can remain dry and comfortable.

Some rabbits will chew their bedding so it is important to ensure that the bedding is safe and will not cause an obstruction if swallowed.

Feed bowls

Feed bowls come in many varying colours, weight and dimensions and should be bought with the rabbit's size in mind. A rabbit's tendency to chew means that plastic bowls should be introduced with caution. Ceramic or metal bowls are the choice of most rabbit keepers as they are robust, easily cleaned and hard to damage. Some rabbit keepers use hoppers that are attached to the outside of the cage with a trough projecting into the cage allowing the owner to feed quickly and efficiently.

Food and treats

Rabbits are very easy to feed and maintain a healthy digestive system as long as they receive enough fibre to keep their digestive system moving. A small amount of a good quality pellet mix and a large quantity of hay on a daily basis, is usually sufficient for most individuals. The provision of vegetable matter such as greens is also important and makes a good treat.

Rabbits do not thrive on sweet foods and should never be fed any food with a high sugary content, such as chocolate. To do so will run the risk of giving the rabbit gut problems such as diarrhoea (for more information, see Chapter 04).

Hayrack

A hayrack is an important purchase both to introduce fibre into the rabbit's diet but also to minimize wastage. Most hayracks attach to the inside of the cage and the rabbit has to pull the hay through the wire. Hayracks help to increase the amount of work that a rabbit does to obtain food and are an excellent way of keeping a rabbit occupied.

Hiding small pieces of vegetable or pellets within the hay will give your rabbit an incentive to consume high quantities of fibre.

Water bottles

Commonly seen in most pet shops, plastic gravity bottles attach onto the outside of the hutch/indoor cage. The rabbit obtains water by pushing its tongue onto the base of the tube and depressing a ball bearing that has been preventing water flow. They should be large enough to provide the rabbit with at least a day's supply of water. There are other options – for example, Ezi-filla bottles are filled through a screw cap at the top of the bottle whilst the bottle stays attached to the outside of the hutch. Some rabbits prefer to drink from bowls and this may be preferable for the larger breeds or as an addition to the water bottle in particularly hot weather. People that keep many rabbits may employ an automatic watering system where plastic piping conveys water into all hutches.

Outdoor run

House or hutch rabbits benefit from a run on grass but, due to the poisonous qualities of some common garden plants and the danger posed by local predators, a protective, enclosed run is a necessary piece of equipment. The run should be well made, heavy and enclosed on all sides but with easy access for the rabbit. The mesh should be thick and strong with no gaps in the mesh itself or the attachment to the frame.

It is also important to ensure that the opening is located somewhere that makes it easy to reach and handle the rabbit. In larger runs, the opening is often quite large and located on the top, in others it is within the side panel. A sheltered area is imperative during hot weather, and can be provided by using a sun brolly with a weighted base. There must also be enough space for the rabbit to be able to run around and kick up its heels. Ideal sizes depend once again on the size of the adult rabbit. Some manufacturers produce collapsible runs that save space when they are not being used.

Litter tray

For an indoor rabbit, at least one litter tray is a necessity. Toilet training requires patience and an understanding of the rabbit's natural behaviour patterns but can be achieved over a short time scale of maybe a few weeks. It is important that the litter tray is bigger than the fully grown rabbit but not so deep that they have a problem jumping in and out. Some litter trays are designed as high-backed corner trays to increase the space that the rabbit has around the tray if it is used in a cage or hutch.

Litter

There are many brands of litter available. It is essential that a non-clumping brand of litter be used as some rabbits have a habit of consuming litter. Whichever litter is first used, it should always be offered and not changed to a different brand every few weeks. Rabbits learn to associate the act of elimination with the substrate that they are eliminating upon (the litter) and long-term the behaviour becomes triggered by the substrate. Changing the litter to a different brand can cause toilet training problems as the trigger is removed.

Toys and enrichment

The outside world is a complex and challenging environment. Inside a hutch or run can become quite predictable so items such as tunnel size pipes, platforms and toys can provide added interest to our rabbits. Toys can be alternated and pipes or platforms can be moved around so that the rabbit keeps using them.

The use of toys by rabbits depends very much on the individual. Some are happy with a cardboard tube; others prefer a cat's bell-ball or a dog's activity ball that dispenses food. The main aim is to provide a variety of items on a rotational basis that stimulate the brain, encourage activity and help to enhance well-being.

Travel box

A sturdy carrying basket will be necessary for trips to the vet or to shows. Most hutch manufacturers or pet stores sell wooden or plastic varieties. If you have a pet rabbit, a basket with a plastic mesh panel at the front (often called a cat basket) is useful should you wish to introduce another rabbit later on, or introduce this rabbit to an existing one. The basket can then be used to allow the individuals access to each other whilst being separated. Being covered at the side is important for trips to the vet when your rabbit will feel very exposed, particularly if you sit next to a dog owner in the waiting room.

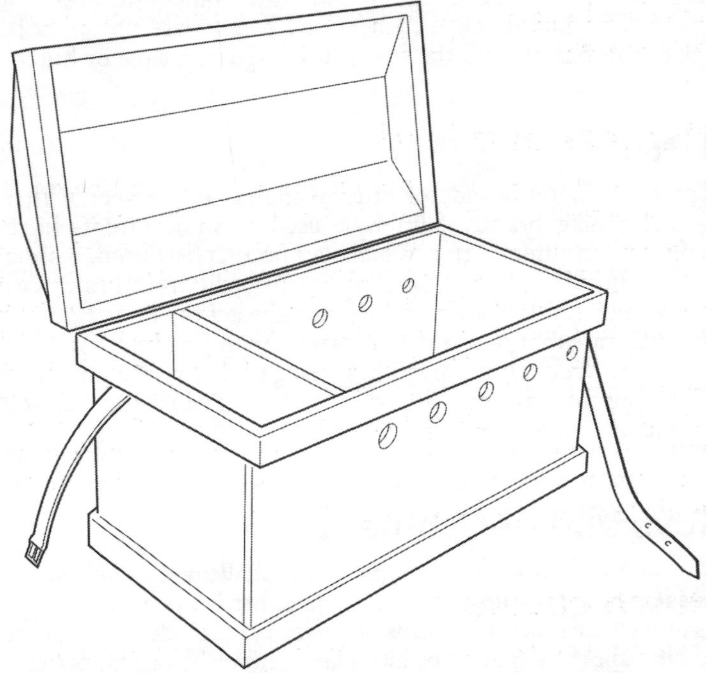

figure 10 typical wooden travel box

Grooming equipment

Rabbits require regular grooming, particularly if they are long-haired, and for this a good-quality metal comb and/or a slicker pad brush (commonly sold in pet stores) will be necessary. A set of small good-quality nail clippers – the size sold for cats is ideal – are needed to keep nails trimmed. Rabbits that have the chance to run around on hardened surfaces require less nail trimming than those living in hutches or on soft ground such as carpets. There is a technique to nail trimming and this is covered in Chapter 06.

Nesting boxes

Based on the natural behaviour of the mother rabbit spending little time with her young (see Chapter 01), nesting boxes enable a hutched doe to have some space away from her kittens. The box has an entrance with a lip that is high enough to keep the babies in for the first few weeks. The nesting box has to be introduced gradually to the doe who may still decide to nest in another corner of the hutch.

Harness and lead

Some owners like to give their rabbits quite a bit of freedom but like them under control; a rabbit harness enables people to take their rabbits for a walk. Harnesses are usually sold with light leads and are fitted around the rabbit's body so that they cannot slip off. Most rabbits will accept a harness after an introduction process that might require some distractions in the form of favourite treats. Encouraging a rabbit to hop on a lead also takes some time and treats but many people are able to take their rabbits out for short 'hops'. Make sure that the harness fits well and is not likely to be chewed by your rabbit. It is also important to keep an eye on your rabbit whilst you are out with them in case they chew through the lead.

Hutch covers

There are some very nice hutch covers available that can help to protect your hutch from the elements. They are usually made of canvas with a roll-down plastic cover to shield the rabbit from rain, sleet and snow. There is a concern that these covers may reduce ventilation so they must be lifted up as soon as the weather has cleared to prevent a temperature rise within the hutch.

Bottle covers

In the winter months, bottles can freeze when the temperature drops making it hard for rabbits to drink. In the summer months, the water bottles can turn green with algae. Although there are many ways of cleaning the algae from bottles (see Chapter 06) it can be prevented from returning by covering the bottle to reduce the light that the algae needs to thrive. Covers can also prevent the water freezing.

Bottle springs

Most water bottles will come with a covered wire that hooks the bottle onto the outside of the hutch but with time, and recurrent use, these can become saggy and unhelpful. Bottle springs, as the name suggests, are long coiled springs that hold the bottle onto the hutch but do not lose their shape (see 'Taking it further' at the back of this book for stockists).

Cleaning equipment

A variety of tools can be used for cleaning rabbits and there is no absolute advice as to the best tools for the job. However, you will need a sturdy dustpan and brush, a metal implement (such as an old garden trowel) to scrape the dirty bedding from the base of the litter tray or hutch and a bucket or other carrier to transport the dirty bedding to the dustbin or the compost heap (for more on composting, see Chapter 06). Some disinfectant, preferably a dry powder (such as Stalosan) is helpful to use in the corner of the hutch or the base of a litter tray.

06 general care

In this chapter you will learn:

- **how to pick up your rabbit**
- **how to trim nails**
- **how to bunny proof your home or garden.**

Handling your rabbit

The rabbit has a very fragile spine that must be supported at all times to prevent back injuries, which can be sustained if they struggle or kick with the back legs. Correct handling of rabbits is vital and is one of the main reasons why young children are not ideal rabbit owners. There are several methods suggested for handling rabbits, which depend on individual preference and the size or previous experience of the rabbit.

The first method is to place one hand behind your rabbit's front legs whilst lifting with the other hand under the rear end (figure 11a). The second method turns the rabbit towards the handler so that the rabbit's head end is steadied. One hand then scoops the rabbit up and takes the weight under the bottom with the other hand placed behind the front legs (figures 11b and c).

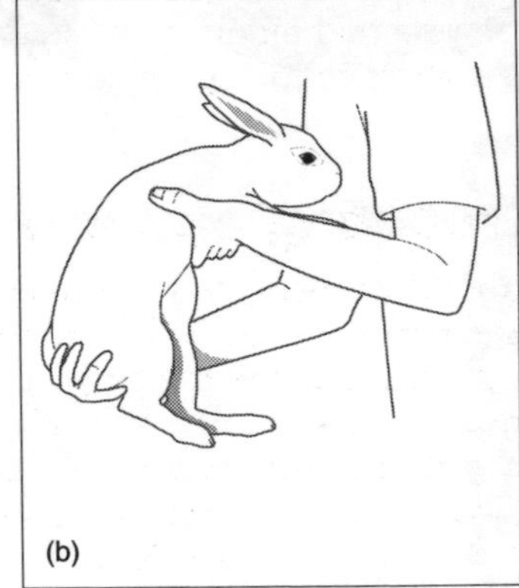

figure 11 three ways to lift a rabbit (b and c most preferable)

Never ever lift your rabbit by the 'scruff' of the neck or the ears as this causes pain and discomfort and mimics the way a rabbit would be carried by a predator, which could cause defensive behaviour. In addition, if the weight of the rabbit is not being supported in both hands, it is not uncommon for them to seriously damage their spines as they try to escape.

Once your rabbit has been picked up it should be placed on your chest or lap in one swift movement. If your rabbit starts to struggle as you pick it up, put it back down, let it calm down and try again later. Never try to force handling on a reluctant rabbit, as this will only increase their apprehension. (If you are having problems picking up your rabbit turn to the section on behaviour problems in Chapter 07.)

Rabbits can start to feel constricted and disorientated as we start to lower them to the floor. To keep your rabbit calm, make sure you are holding him correctly and try to cover his eyes with your hand or the crook of your arm.

Grooming and moult

Rabbits are meticulous groomers and are thought to spend some 16 per cent of their daily activity in grooming. Wild rabbits need to ensure that their coat is well maintained all year round to protect them against the elements as well as to prevent infestations from fleas, lice and mites. The coat of the wild rabbit is much shorter and denser than many of our breeds and does not knot easily. Rabbits are able to use their incisors to remove any dead hair.

There are areas of the body that rabbits are unable to reach and for this they rely on other rabbits. For domestic rabbits, if they do not have a companion rabbit, they rely on us. Grooming your rabbit regularly is an easy way to get to know the feel of your rabbit's body so that you notice any changes quickly. The aim of grooming is also to remove any dead hair and prevent the development of knots in the fur.

Long-haired rabbits require daily grooming by their owners. This is a major consideration to anyone taking on breeds such as the Angora, Swiss Fox, Cashmere Lop or Lionhead. Not grooming a long-haired rabbit regularly will lead to matted fur that becomes uncomfortable for the rabbit, dirty and then infected. This is a serious problem if flies lay their eggs in this matted hair as maggots will burrow into the skin – causing fly strike, an often fatal condition.

If you find any knots in your rabbit's fur do not pull them out. Rabbit skin tears easily so you may damage your rabbit. Instead, start opening the knot from the top using your fingers and removing a small piece at a time. If you are not planning to show your rabbit then clip the hair away gradually and keep the coat shorter during the warmer months.

Short-haired rabbits need occasional grooming by their owners, usually as they go into moult. Juvenile rabbits have their first moult between six and eight months of age when their adult coat will develop and they will shed the baby coat. From then on, rabbits usually have two moults a year (although rabbits that live indoors may not moult as the temperature within the home is controlled).

Rabbits build up a thick coat to help them maintain their body temperature during the colder winter months and shed this during the spring in time for the warmer months. The summer coat is much finer than the winter coat to enable them to stay cool and is replaced towards the end of autumn. If the seasonal change over from spring to summer or autumn to winter takes a long time, rabbits may appear to be in an almost continuous moult until the weather stabilizes.

Moult usually starts at the head and moves along the body leaving the new hair behind it. As hair is composed of a protein (called keratin), it is important to feed a healthy diet to a rabbit undergoing moult.

There are other times when rabbits can lose their fur that are not associated with moult. A pregnant female or a rabbit undergoing a phantom pregnancy may pluck the fur from her chest to line a nest (for more information, see Chapter 08). Rabbits can over-groom themselves or their companions leading to bald and sore patches; this is often due to a lack of fibre in the diet or teeth problems so it is worth having a chat with your vet (for more information see also Chapters 04 and 07).

Ears

Rabbits can usually keep the outsides and insides of their ears clean by themselves using their paws and some saliva – watching a rabbit clean its ears is a great time waster!

It is worth checking inside the ear canal as part of your regular checks (see below) to ensure that there are no scabs or crusts, redness or sore areas which might suggest mites or an infection. A wipe around the ear canal with a small amount of cotton wool soaked in warm water is sufficient to clean the ear flap and the outer ear canal, but never poke down into the ear itself as this might cause some damage.

Make an appointment to visit the vet if you are concerned by any signs of soreness or discharge.

Teeth

The teeth of the rabbit grow continuously and need to be worn down by regular grazing. A healthy diet (see Chapter 04) should wear them efficiently unless the teeth do not meet when the rabbit has its mouth closed. These rabbits are said to have malocclusion and the rabbit is unable to eat properly or consume the caecotrophs (faeces) that it produces. Other signs that the teeth may be causing problems include wet fur around and under the mouth, weeping eyes, fur plucking and lots of faeces stuck around the rabbit's bottom. After a while the rabbit may be physically unable to eat so another sign is a lack of interest in food and weight loss.

If left unchecked, maloccluded teeth will continue growing, which can prove fatal for the rabbit (for more information, see Chapter 10).

Nail trimming

Rabbits that are running around on concrete regularly should wear their nails down but most rabbits need their nails trimmed every few months. Rabbit nails are very similar to ours with 'dead' white tips and pink areas that have a blood supply. Ideally there should be 5mm between the pink area and the end of the nail itself. The differentiation of the nail can be clearly seen in natural light but a torch may be needed to provide a backlight for dark nails.

The easiest way to trim a rabbit's nails is to turn the rabbit on its back and cradle it in the crook of your arm so that the bases of the feet are uppermost. Each foot can be held by the hand of the arm that is holding the rabbit whilst the clippers are held in

figure 12 trimming nails

the free hand. If you are unsure about clipping nails, start by taking off a small amount of nail and do this regularly until you gain some confidence and your rabbit becomes used to the procedure. Laying a towel over your rabbit's body whilst you do each foot can prevent your rabbit scratching you if he or she struggles.

An alternative method, for a rabbit that struggles when it is laid on its back, is for one person to hold them in a corner with a hand placed gently over the shoulder blades and their head facing away from any walls. The other person can lift each foot forward and trim the nails, using the tip of a finger under the foot to spread the pads of the feet making the nails easier to reach. The rabbit can then be turned around to do the other side.

If a nail is trimmed too close and starts to bleed, pressing some cotton wool or tissue may stem the bleeding. Styptic powder (available from pet shops) or cornflour can stop bleeding.

Bottoms

If rabbits have faeces and matted hair around their bottoms they are likely to be uncomfortable and run the risk of attracting flies in the warmer months. The flies can lay eggs on the rabbit's fur and the maggots will burrow into the rabbit causing a potentially fatal condition called fly strike.

To prevent flystrike, ensure the following:

- Feed your rabbit a diet of predominantly hay to ensure that it is healthy and to keep its weight down. It is important that your rabbit consumes the first set of sticky faeces that it produces (caecotrophs) and that teeth are kept in good condition so that it is able to consume these faeces.
- If your rabbit is overweight, reduce its food ration and increase the amount of hay that it eats (hay is 'low calorie' so they can eat plenty). An overweight rabbit will not be able to reach round and consume the first set of faeces which means that it will get stuck on its bottom or hind legs.
- Check your rabbit's bottom regularly (more so during the warmer months) by turning it on its back. If there is any mess around the area, remove it with some cotton wool.
- If you have a long-haired rabbit, groom it every day to prevent mats developing. Matted hair causes discomfort to the rabbit and traps faeces. If necessary, clip the fur around the rabbit's bottom carefully using small round-ended scissors with long slim blades and then apply some Veterinary Wound Powder as an antiseptic fly repellent.
- Deter flies and other flying insects with herbs and use sticky fly papers to reduce numbers (for more information, see Discouraging pests and flies on p.73).

Washing rabbits

It is rarely necessary to bathe a rabbit, and this should only be done with extreme caution as rabbits can find the experience very distressing. Rabbits are very good at grooming themselves but if there is a problem with a particular area, such as compacted faeces on a rabbit's bottom, then bathing just that area is acceptable. The rabbit should not be immersed in the water and should be held firmly by one person, perhaps wrapped in a towel, whilst another person washes the affected area.

Rabbit fur can take a long time to dry and a hairdryer held at quite a way from the rabbit's body may not cause too much distress. Dry shampoos can be used to remove stains to the base of feet.

If you are planning to exhibit your rabbit, be wary of washing away dirty patches on the body or feet too close to the show as some rabbit fur can curl once it has been washed. In addition, if you use a perfumed product to remove dirty smells you will draw attention to your rabbit, which might be frowned on by the judge!

Cleaning out litter trays and hutches

Rabbit hutches and litter trays should be emptied and cleaned thoroughly once a week but in the summer months damp dirty bedding should be removed every two to three days to deter flies. A powdered disinfectant can help to remove odours whilst absorbing any urine and this can be sprinkled into the base of the litter tray or toileting corner of the hutch. There are also spray disinfectants that can be helpful but some may contain little active ingredient. A good scrub with a warm solution of a biological washing powder or liquid will remove urine odours from both hutches and indoor furnishings.

Water bottles should be cleaned once a week with some warm water, a bottlebrush and washing-up liquid. They must be thoroughly rinsed before refilling and attaching to the hutch. For heavily stained bottles, or for a 'spring clean', use a sterilizing fluid suitable for babies' bottles, leaving the bottles to soak for the specified amount of time before rinsing thoroughly. There are some products on the market to help reduce the build up of algae during the summer months; one such is Aviclens by Dr Squiggles. Alternatively, bottle covers can reduce the amount of light reaching the water and also prevent the build of of algae.

Litter trays can become quite stained and will need a regular clean with a hose and a brush. A rinse with some disinfectant prior to refilling with shavings will help deter flies and prevent infections.

Regular checks

If your rabbit is living in the house it is easy to see any changes in behaviour, movement and routine, but if your rabbit is living outside this may be harder to spot, so it is sensible to set time aside for regular health checks.

Daily checks

Try to see your rabbit at the same time each day so that you will know very quickly if there is a problem. Ask yourself the following questions to be sure that he or she is healthy and not in any discomfort:

- Has your rabbit eaten all the food you would have expected for this time of day?
- Has your rabbit drunk as much water as usual?
- Does your rabbit's body feel normal when you run your hands over it?
- Are there lots of hard faeces in the toilet corner?
- Is your rabbit moving freely and as energetically as you would expect at this time of the day?
- Is your rabbit behaving normally?

If you answer 'no' to any of these questions, check on your rabbit again within two hours to see if the answers are any different. If not, then take your rabbit to see a vet.

Weekly checks

A weekly check of your rabbit should be more of an overall health assessment. The following list is a guideline for assessing your rabbit's physical condition:

- When cleaning out your rabbit's living area look for anything unusual in the appearance of the urine or faeces.
- Check your rabbit's back end for any evidence of diarrhoea or trapped faeces (in the summer months this should be done everyday to prevent fly strike).
- If you have a rabbit with short or medium-length hair, groom them to remove dead hair and prevent the development of tangles (a long-haired rabbit should be groomed daily).
- Check inside your rabbit's ears.
- Check your rabbit's mouth, eyes and around the dewlap (under the chin) for any signs of wetness that might indicate tooth problems.
- Brush over the hutch doorframes and around the mesh to remove any debris. Unless you have a phobia of spiders, remember that they help to reduce the number of flies around the hutch so cobwebs could improve the health of your rabbit!

Monthly checks

Once a month your rabbit needs an 'MOT' to help it maintain good health:

- Check your rabbit's nails and clip them if necessary (see section above).
- Holding the rabbit's head gently, part the mouth to check the teeth and mouth.
- Check the rabbit's coat for any dandruff and check the skin for any scabs. Run your hand backwards and forwards over the rabbit's coat to see how it feels. By doing this, you should also feel any lumps or bumps on your rabbit's body.
- If you have a male rabbit that has not been neutered, check his testicles for any signs of swelling or redness.
- If you have a rabbit that wears a show ring around its leg, check that the ring is loose and can be turned through 360° with your finger and thumb. (For more information on show rings see Chapter 09. If there is a problem with the ring turn to Chapter 10 for guidelines on removing the ring.)
- If your rabbit lives in a hutch, check the hutch for any signs of wear and tear or damage, particularly internally. Tighten any loose catches or hinges and fix any loose joints.
- Clean the floor of the hutch or indoor cage with a warm solution of biological washing powder to remove the odour of faeces or urine. Leave to dry before applying a disinfectant and fresh bedding.

Every six months

Similar to the spring clean that we do to our homes, twice a year we should give an outdoor rabbit's home environment a touch-up and the rabbit itself a proper health check.

- Re-varnish the outside of the rabbit's hutch (using a weatherproof, animal-friendly stain).
- Check the roof of the hutch is firmly attached and waterproof, replacing the felt if necessary (rolls of mineral felt are available from builders' merchants and hardware stores).
- With the inside of the hutch clean and dry and the rabbit in another location for several hours, coat the floor and several inches up each wall with a fast drying bituminous paint to protect the wood from moisture. Pay particular attention to your rabbit's toilet area.

- Visit your vet for your rabbit's Myxomatosis and VHD booster vaccinations and a general health check.

Disposal of manure

Rabbit manure is very high in nitrogen and contains phosphoric acid and potash making it an excellent addition to a compost bin or when applied directly to the base of plants. In some circles it is thought to be the best natural manure for the garden.

Composting reduces waste, improves soil and is an easy way to remove large quantities of rabbit waste. Grass clippings, leaves, tea bags, egg shells, coffee grounds, uncooked vegetable peelings, rabbit pellets and urine soaked shavings or straw are all acceptable items for the compost. Its high nitrogen content means that rabbit urine and droppings and the carbon-rich bedding material help speed up the rate of decomposition. Wood shavings, straw and hay, shredded paper and cardboard products are all really good for composting. Even the rabbit's hair can be composted, although it might take a while to decompose.

As rabbit droppings are dry, it is important to include lots of green material (such as vegetable peelings and grass cuttings) to keep the compost moist. Some composting organizations recommend watering the straw or hay before it is added to the bin.

For keen gardeners, it can take anything from 6 to 24 months to produce a fine, sweet-smelling compost, but the process is ongoing from that point with a regular supply of environmentally-friendly, home grown compost.

Many local councils in the UK provide special bins for the collection of material that is appropriate for composting but they may list rabbit manure as an exclusion under 'animal waste' – if you have large quantities of rabbit manure each week, contact your local allotment or horticultural society to see if any of their members are interested in collecting a regular supply.

Discouraging pests and flies

Keeping rabbits outside can encourage mice, rats and flying insects to the garden, species that are naturally attracted to areas offering food and shelter. However, in the interests of preventing disease and health risks to your rabbit they should be discouraged.

Here are some tips:

- Keep all food and hay in secure metal or heavy plastic containers and ensure lids are replaced correctly after use.
- Sweep the floor around the hutches after cleaning and discard any waste food in a bin away from the rabbit hutch.
- If you keep your rabbit, or its food, in an outside shed make sure that it is in good repair with no holes or loose tiles that rodents can enter through.
- Keeping a cat or dog helps discourage rodents.
- Keeping spiders alive and not brushing away cobwebs can reduce the number of flies and biting insects.
- Green netting (available from agricultural or garden stores) can be used to cover the windows or doors of sheds or to provide a screen over the hutch whilst allowing ventilation.
- There are spot-on treatments available to prevent parasites (such as mites and lice) living on rabbits – these are available from your vet or pet shop.
- Regular cleaning and disinfecting of hutches should make the rabbit home less attractive to flies that like damp, smelly environments.
- Biting insects and flies can be discouraged by spraying citronella on the outside of the hutch or planting herbs such as lavender, rosemary, mint and thyme near the rabbit hutch. Hanging dried bunches of herbs near the hutch is also recommended as a natural deterrent.
- Due to the potential threat of fly strike to our rabbits, if there are lots of flies around the hutch you may need to consider hanging sticky fly strips near the hutch. If your rabbits live in a shed then an electric fly killer can reduce numbers or introduce a liquid flytrap if you don't like the sound of the electrocutions!
- If you become infested with mice or rats, there are humane traps available from hardware shops and garden centres.

Keeping mind and body healthy

To maintain a healthy body requires a healthy diet – high in fibre to maintain the flow of the rabbit's unusual digestive process and to keep the teeth neatly worn. The rabbit also requires regular exercise to maintain strong bones, muscle tone and trim nails. Regular health checks should be completed so that any signs of diarrhoea, breathing difficulties, and general lethargy or teeth problems can be treated quickly.

Social contact

In the wild, rabbits live in small groups, and our pet rabbits require similar company too. If we are prepared to spend at least a couple of hours a day with the rabbit, we can be their companion. Of course this is easier if the rabbit lives in the home permanently or comes into the home for short periods of time each day. For a variety of reasons, people are not always able to be the best companion to their rabbit and in these cases keeping a pair of rabbits is the ideal solution.

If you obtain two rabbits at the same time then the relationship should settle down and both individuals are likely to bond with each other. If you have a single rabbit that you would like to get a companion for, time must be taken to ensure that the introduction of another rabbit does not cause stress to either individual. A rabbit of the opposite sex is most likely to make a successful companion than a rabbit of the same sex as the rabbits might start to become competitive around the breeding season. This is covered in more detail in two other chapters of this book – see Chapters 03 and 07.

In practice, another rabbit means doubling the space allowance and providing as many areas as possible for the rabbits to hide in so that if they need some time apart they are able to have it. Cardboard boxes, plastic tunnels and raised areas can all help.

Exercise requirements

In the wild, the majority of the time spent outside the burrow is spent grazing. Rabbits are continually on the move but as their food – vegetation – is stationary, they do not need to expend a lot of energy. However, rabbits are able to exhibit a great turn of speed when they feel under threat and need to return to the burrow as quickly as possible. In the course of their normal life, wild rabbits spend time relaxing and interacting socially, obtaining food and avoiding being eaten.

Our domestic rabbits still need long periods of time hopping around and exploring as if they were grazing. This may involve standing up on their back legs or hopping around on all fours. This is why the space requirements for hutches state that they need to be higher than the rabbit at full stretch and long enough for them to take several good hops in any direction. Ideally a rabbit should be allowed to run within the home, a fenced-in portion of the garden, a covered outdoor run or the inside of a shed for at least an hour every day.

Rabbits, particularly young ones, often have a mad dash around the enclosed area, quite literally dashing around and twisting in mid-air. This is perfectly normal and is simply their way of letting off steam.

Rabbits that have always lived within a hutch should be given high levels of freedom with caution. A rabbit's bones can be quite brittle and a lack of exercise during development can increase this – any sudden dashes or leaps may cause significant damage. Exercise should be introduced very gradually to these individuals.

Environmental enrichment

It is hard work keeping the mind and body of a domestic rabbit active but it is imperative to maintain well-being and avoid problems. Comparing the behaviour of the European wild rabbit, our rabbit's closest ancestor, with that of domestic rabbits highlights some major differences in activity levels and behaviour patterns that can cause problems.

Wild rabbits are continually alert and on the move. Whilst it is less stressful for our domestic rabbit to be protected from predators and fed on a regular regime, steps need to be taken to ensure that inactivity does not lead to boredom, as this can lead to behavioural problems such as extremely destructive behaviour.

There are no hard and fast rules for rabbit activities – use your imagination. Simple changes, such as increasing the three-dimensional feel to the enclosure or area that your rabbit has access to, can have a profound effect. Raised or hidden areas, tunnels, barriers or hanging items can change an environment from a flat piece of flooring into a maze of interest.

Occasional treats can be given to elicit some activity from your rabbit – perhaps they are hidden or hung slightly out of the rabbit's reach. As rabbits spend long periods of time grazing in the wild, they should be given as much as possible to chew each day – unlimited access to hay, perhaps fruit tree branches or even old cardboard boxes.

Many rabbits, particularly solitary rabbits, are highly playful and enjoy throwing items such as toddlers' teething rings or chasing cat toys. Some rabbits become very adept at releasing food from puzzle toys designed for dogs (such as activity balls or Buster Cubes) and others make great football players. To keep rabbits playful, whilst maximizing your attempts to keep the rabbit's mind active, toys should be rotated so that each one remains 'interesting'.

A word of caution – if your rabbit has been leading a non-stimulating life and, after reading this book, you decide to make some changes, do so gradually. Suddenly giving him lots of freedom, introducing another rabbit and filling the hutch with boxes and tubes might cause stress and be counter-productive in the short term.

Bunny-proofing your home and garden

Rabbit owners have to accept that is perfectly normal for rabbits to chew and dig, sometimes for long periods of time or during particular times of the year (such as the breeding season). Problems arise when rabbits are not given enough access to substrates that it is acceptable for them to dig and chew so they turn their destruction onto inappropriate items.

The items most likely to be damaged are electrical cables, wallpaper, wooden items such as chair legs, books, flowerbeds, lawns and carpets. Adequate 'bunny-proofing' combines denying access to certain areas with protecting items that the rabbit regularly comes into contact with. However, denying the opportunity does not solve the problem – rabbits must be given alternatives to chew or dig into.

Electrical cables can be covered using a snap-on plastic cover called conduit from DIY/hardware stores or they can be lifted out of the rabbit's reach. Aquatic centres sell special tubing for fish tanks in various colours and sizes which can be threaded over the wires once the plug is removed. If the plug is moulded to the wire, split the tubing along the length and push the wire through.

Wallpaper can be covered with screw-on Perspex sheeting or access to rooms with wallpaper can be denied altogether. Chair legs and other wooden items can be treated with a taste deterrent, such as bitter apple spray or eucalyptus oil, or moved out of harm's way. Books and other items, such as magazines or telephone directories should be placed out of reach – remember that rabbits can reach quite high when they stand on their back legs!

Some houseplants and many outdoor plants can be dangerous to rabbits. From the rabbit's point of view, a flowerbed or lawn provides a wonderful area for grazing, rooting around and tunnel digging. To avoid having a sick rabbit and a decimated garden, have areas of the garden out of bounds, use an enclosed rabbit run or plant only rabbit-friendly plants and expect them to be nibbled or dug up from time to time.

A large amount of digging often occurs in the corners of rooms or behind pieces of furniture leading to significant amounts of damage to carpets or other floor coverings. Whilst blocking off areas can prevent damage, the problem will still remain unless an alternative area is provided – perhaps a cardboard box lined with something sturdy such as a piece of lino and then covered with sand or soil. Ask your local carpet warehouse to give you their unwanted large cardboard tubes and place one behind the sofa to give your rabbit a long tunnel as well as an area to dig in, rather than the back of your sofa.

It is normal for female rabbits to start digging at the onset of the natural breeding season in early spring. This is the time when nesting sites and burrows would be prepared for the young and is not a behavioural problem, as such. Neutering can help females that dig at this time of year.

Rabbits that chew excessively are often lacking fibre in their diet and are literally grazing – this can be directed to non-food items including another rabbit's fur. Assuming that the rabbit has healthy teeth, the diet should be adapted to contain much more natural fibre in the form of hay and some green vegetables (for further information see Chapter 04).

Hot weather

Rabbits can usually cope with a wide range of temperatures if they are well ventilated. As rabbits are unable to control their body temperature by panting or sweating, the ears act as heat regulators, lowering the overall blood temperature by increasing the blood flow through the large surface area. You may also notice your rabbit lying on a cold floor in the home or moving bedding in the hutch to expose the cooler base.

There are specific problems that may occur during hot weather:

- Transporting rabbits during hot weather should only be done during the coolest times of the day, preferably in a car with air conditioning or another form of good ventilation. Rabbits should be travelled in boxes that have air vents on top and preferably on one side to allow the flow of air. The use of cardboard boxes is not advised, as people tend to rely on air flowing through the flaps of the box rather than cutting holes into the sides. If you have to take a long journey during hot weather, stop regularly to give the rabbits some air and do not stack boxes on top of each other. Try to ensure that each box has at least 30mm of space around each side but avoid the temptation to spread the boxes out, as they will become unsafe should you need to brake suddenly.

- Assuming that the rabbit's hutch is placed in a cool shaded area of the garden and the rabbit has a continual supply of water, then the rabbit should be able to maintain its temperature. However, if the temperature within the shed or home goes above 35°C, then you may need to introduce sun shades, electric fans, or to move the hutch somewhere cooler (particularly in the home when the sun coming through a glass window can cause a large increase in the temperature). A sun brolly with a weighted base can be used to shield a hutch or run from hot sunshine.
- If your rabbit appears to have become distressed by the heat (outward signs include breathing through the mouth, struggling to breathe, convulsions and weakness) you must spray your rabbit with water as soon as possible to reduce its body temperature. If all else fails spraying the rabbit with cool water, but not covering the head, should help to improve their condition before they are taken to a vet who will address the dehydration problems associated with heat stroke.
- There is an increase in the number of flies and biting associated with the warmer months. To prevent the risk of fly strike or Myxomatosis, rabbits should be cleaned out regularly and vaccinated at least once a year (your vet will advise on this). There are tips on how to reduce the number of flies earlier in this chapter.

Holiday care

When you go on holiday will need to find someone that can come round and look after your rabbit. It is important that the daily routine stays as similar as possible so that your rabbit is fed, exercised and checked in the manner that it is used to.

Finding someone reliable is often quite difficult but there is usually a member of the family, a neighbour or a friend happy to help so that your rabbit can stay in their home environment, whilst you can be sure that it will be fed well and safe. There are pet sitters who may advertise in your veterinary practice, telephone directory or local paper – they come round to your house each day to look after your animals for a daily fee. Another avenue is a boarding establishment, as some kennels and catteries have started to take small animals and some exclusively lodge rabbits and guinea pigs.

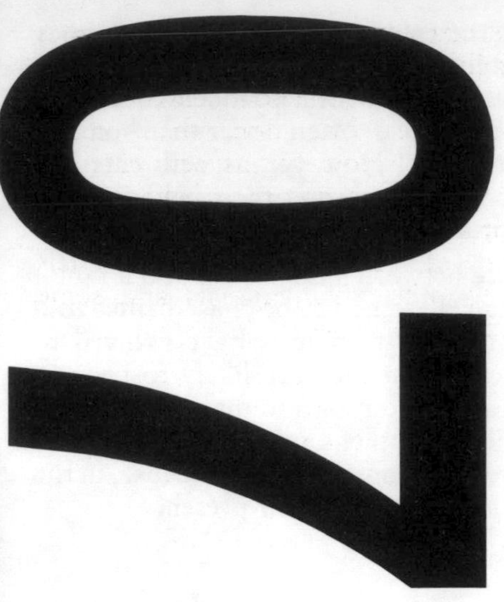

rabbit behaviour

In this chapter you will learn:

- **how to interpret normal behaviour**
- **how rabbits learn**
- **how to solve behaviour problems.**

Although the intelligence of the rabbit is often questioned, they exhibit all the bonding characteristics of the larger companion animals. They can be trained to toilet in a particular location, walk on a lead and come when called, often better than some of their canine or feline counterparts! However, as with cats and dogs, problems can arise if we misinterpret their behaviour or interact with them inappropriately.

The most important difference between a dog or cat and a rabbit is that rabbits are prey animals, designed to be chased and avoid being eaten. Many of the rabbit's responses have evolved to prevent predation – this means that they are likely to become scared, they may try to run away from us and may not respond in the way that we expect. For example, a rabbit in pain is more likely to sit still than to move about and vocalize, because, in the wild, the latter would alert a predator to their presence.

Normal behaviour

An animal's behaviour indicates a variety of emotions and motivations. To truly appreciate a rabbit, and be able to gain the most from your relationship with it, an understanding of their natural behaviour is vital.

A list of the most common behaviours and their meanings is as follows:

Aggression – aggressive behaviour may involve a threat (no contact) or an attack (contact). The rabbit may grunt and use its front feet, hind legs or teeth during aggression.

Allogrooming – occurs when one rabbit grooms another. This behaviour is often used to strengthen relationships and appears as licking and light nibbling if directed towards the owner.

Chasing – rabbits often chase each other during disputes over territory or during courtship. Occasionally they may chase each other for fun!

Chewing (no food) – if a rabbit moves its jaw so that it looks as though it is chewing but it is not eating then the rabbit is probably very relaxed.

Chin rubbing – rabbits mark anything that doesn't smell of them with the scent glands that are located under the chin. They may even repeatedly mark items as the scent fades. In the wild this behaviour lets other rabbits know whose territory they have entered – in the home the behaviour may be seen around new items of furniture or even the owner's legs.

Circling – female rabbits circle male rabbits during courtship and this is often combined with some grunting. When a rabbit is kept alone this behaviour can be directed towards the owner and is most apparent during spring and early summer (the rabbit's natural breeding season).

Digging – female rabbits dig the majority of the burrows in the wild and males help out a little. In a domestic situation a male or female rabbit might dig up the lawn, carpets or flowerbeds.

Elimination – the act of excreting waste products from the body in the form of urine or faeces. Rabbits produce two sets of faeces – the first of which are called caecotrophs and are re-digested by the rabbit. The second faeces are dry and hard and are left in areas called latrines.

Enurination – male rabbits spray females with a jet of urine during courtship.

Fighting – actual combat between rabbits is quite rare as many fights are prevented by the displays of parallel runs and jumps that precede a confrontation. These displays signal the size and strength of the individual, which allows either party to decide if it is worth proceeding. Fights occur more readily in domestic situations where space is limited, resources (such as food) are concentrated into one area and there is little room to avoid each other.

Foot thumping – rabbits thump their feet quite rapidly to alert the rest of the group to danger. Domestic rabbits – even living alone – may do this if they feel under threat.

Fur Plucking – generally speaking this is a sign of a pregnancy, or a phantom pregnancy. A female rabbit plucks the hair from her chest to line a nest made from bedding. In some situations rabbits pull their own hair out or over-groom a companion through stress, teeth problems, boredom or a lack of fibre in their diet.

Grazing – rabbits consume their food by grazing which involves continuously taking in small amounts of vegetation over long periods. There is voracious grazing when the rabbit has its head down for long periods of time and zigzag grazing interspersed with breaks to scan the horizon for threats. In a domestic situation this behaviour is rarely seen over such long periods as rabbits are fed concentrated food from bowls and have limited access to grass and vegetation.

Grooming – rabbits groom themselves to maintain condition and hygiene. Long periods of time will be spent cleaning every area of the body using the mouth and paws. Another rabbit will groom the areas that can't be reached during periods of allogrooming.

Growling – rabbits growl when they feel threatened. This may occur between individuals or towards owners when they approach the rabbit suddenly or put a hand into the rabbit's territory.

Grunting – rabbits grunt during courtship rituals such as circling.

Hopping – rabbits are said to 'hop' and this is the rabbit's main mode of locomotion when it is relaxed. The long hind legs and spine facilitate hopping.

Jumping/Friskiness – rabbits can often be seen to leap around, twisting in mid-air. This is usually their attempt at letting off steam, but may occur more when they are young or during the breeding season.

Lying – rabbits lie down on their sides with their back legs extended when they are relaxed. On warm days they may lie this way on cool surfaces.

Marking – rabbits mark poignant areas of their territory with urine, faeces and chin wipes to indicate boundaries to rival groups. Individuals may also be anointed to give the group a common smell. In the home, rabbits will often 'chin' pieces of furniture and may urinate or leave faeces on anything new.

Mating – the male 'flirts' with the female by circling her and grunting and she may receive the occasional spray of urine. The copulation is brief and the male holds the female by biting her neck. The act of mating leads to the release of an egg by the female, which is then fertilized by the male's sperm. This is an unusual system of ovulation within mammals.

Nipping – rabbits can nip during aggressive encounters or at times when they feel under conflict. Occasionally they nip their owner in an affectionate manner, but this is usually misplaced, or misunderstood, allogrooming.

Parenting – rabbits have an unusual system of parenting called absentee care. The young are kept in a separate nest site with the entrance blocked to keep them safe from predators and their mother feeds them once every twenty hours. In domestic situations, mothers are usually with their kittens permanently due to hutch design but can be removed for short periods once the kittens are three weeks old.

Pregnancy – the gestation period for a rabbit is around thirty days. Towards the middle of the pregnancy the doe starts to prepare a suitable nest area, which she then lines with hair from her chest during the last week of gestation.

Refection – the act of consuming the first set of faeces (caecotrophs). The rabbit reaches around to the anus to consume them as they are excreted. This usually happens during daylight hours when the rabbit would be in its burrow.

Scraping – similar to digging, rabbits will perform this behaviour to create a scrape (a shallow indentation in the earth) to lie in. If the rabbit has not been spayed this behaviour can indicate that she is looking for a potential nest site.

Spraying – male rabbits tend to spray urine to mark areas within the territory or during courtship when a female will be sprayed with a small amount of urine. Male rabbits develop a pecking order between themselves and spraying can be used to reinforce their status. In domestic homes, both sexes can urinate on items, owners or each other.

Tooth grinding – the rabbit may be in pain.

Tonic immobility – when a rabbit is caught by a predator or feels itself to be in immediate danger it will exhibit tonic immobility; in other words it will 'play dead'. The rabbit is, however, conscious. Many people will 'trance' a rabbit by placing it on its back, which enables them to examine the rabbit or trim its nails without the rabbit struggling. It is not something that should be done for fun and there is evidence to suggest that it is a highly stressful state (see Chapter 11).

Scream – rabbits scream when they are under severe threat or in extreme pain.

Training

Rabbits are able to learn many behaviours, from litter training through to recall.

How rabbits learn

Classical conditioning: this form of learning occurs when a stimulus – such as a sound or sight – that is unimportant becomes significant because it leads to something meaningful happening and then triggers an involuntary action. Rabbits learn that the sound of the back door opening as we come into the garden precedes being fed at certain times of the day. This sound can then cause rabbits to come to the front of the hutch and wait to be fed.

Classical conditioning can be used to trigger a response from an animal, which it has no control over. This is useful for litter training where the litter or litter tray becomes the conditioned (i.e. learned) stimulus that causes the response of eliminating urine or faeces.

Operant conditioning: also known as trial and error learning, is a very common way for animals to learn. In essence they learn to repeat or avoid behaviours depending on the outcome. So if a rabbit approaches its owner and this behaviour receives a positive outcome (such as a treat or a stroke), then the behaviour will be repeated.

Desensitization is a technique used to teach a rabbit to associate something it doesn't like with a positive experience. This can take place if a rabbit does not like being handled but is taught to accept it when it leads to something nice (see below).

Timing

The timing of a response to behaviour must occur at the time of the action itself to have any effect. In other words, if a rabbit is doing a behaviour that we would like to see again then the rabbit must be rewarded as that behaviour occurs. A few seconds later is a few seconds too late and can mean that the rabbit takes longer to learn or learns the wrong thing.

Rewards

Like most animals, rabbits can learn that some of our phrases and interactions are rewarding. Stroking, praising and scratching the flat area between the rabbit's eyes are all examples of interactions that our rabbits would consider to be pleasant.

Of course, food acts as a reward. Throughout this book, the importance of a healthy diet has been highlighted and food rewards can include a small piece of a favourite vegetable, herb or hay-based snacks.

Punishment

A negative consequence to behaviour can prevent it from occurring again but punishment should never involve physical contact, particularly in a prey animal such as the rabbit that will view us as a very large threat and avoid future contact. Some rabbits will continue performing a behaviour despite continuous reprimands because receiving good or bad attention is better than receiving no attention at all – so punishment can also be a reward.

The easiest and most effective way to change behaviour is to deal with the cause rather than the symptom – ignore it, learn why it is happening and take steps to prevent it happening next time.

Litter training

The natural instinct of a wild rabbit to use one area as its latrine is still true in our domestic pets. We can utilize this to let them live in the home or to make cleaning out the hutch easier, by training them to use a litter tray. The following step by step programme should litter train your rabbit effectively; if you have a problem read the section on behaviour problems later in this chapter.

- Confine your rabbit to a suitably small area for a period of three to four days. In the home, an indoor cage should be used, but for an outdoor rabbit the hutch itself is sufficient.
- Provide food, water and toys and cover the floor area with bedding such as newspaper, wood shavings or straw. This helps your rabbit to gain a sense of security in one environment and should lead to the rabbit choosing a particular corner as the latrine.
- Once this has been achieved a litter tray – or other suitable receptacle – can be filled with some of the rabbit's soiled bedding.
- Rabbits often deposit faeces whilst they are grazing so placing a hayrack or food bowl at the end of the litter tray can aid this process. In the early days a food reward, such as a small piece of a vegetable, can be given to the rabbit each time it jumps into the tray.
- After a couple of days a non-clumping brand of litter can be introduced to the tray. The amount of litter in the tray can then be increased each day.

- The litter tray should not be cleaned out too often for the first few weeks so that the scent of faeces/urine remains long enough to keep encouraging the rabbit to return to the tray.
- Once toilet training has occurred, a thorough clean-out once every few days is acceptable but this may need to be increased during the summer months to prevent the attraction of flies.

Preventing behaviour problems

Many behaviour problems can be prevented by ensuring that our rabbits are kept in a safe environment, with plenty of space, a good diet and regular social contact. The checklist below pinpoints key areas of rabbit husbandry that can help prevent, or address, a behaviour problem. Your rabbit should:

- have areas to retreat to if it is scared or wants to be left alone
- be free from the presence of predators, unusual noises and smells
- be able to dig and work to gain food
- be able to mark its territory effectively with chin secretions, urine and faecal pellets
- not feel threatened, at any time
- feel secure when picked up and not 'loomed over' by the owner
- be fed an appropriate diet that encourages normal digestive function, dental abrasion and prolonged feeding time
- have regular exercise and social contact with another individual
- not be encountering reprimands or punishment.

Early experience

Socializing a rabbit and habituating it to its environment is one of the most important steps in its early development and one that can help prevent behaviour problems developing later in life. As rabbits can live for five to ten years, it is important to make these years as enjoyable as possible for you and your rabbit.

In essence, a rabbit borne into a noisy, healthy environment that encounters several different people (and perhaps other animals) on a daily basis is more likely to develop into a relaxed animal unlikely to display fear-related behaviours as an adult. A rabbit borne into a quiet, sheltered environment with little contact with the outside world may develop into a nervous adult who avoids all contact with its owner.

Although behaviourists have not yet pinpointed the sensitive period in a rabbit's development, studies suggest that experiences the rabbit has between ten days and six weeks of age can have a profound impact on their later behaviour. There are several studies that suggest handling rabbit kittens between ten and twenty days of age affects behaviour and leads to bolder and less fearful rabbits when 14 weeks old. Handling rabbits at the age of three months may also have an impact on their response to humans as an adult. One interesting piece of research showed that only rabbits that had been handled by humans before weaning (just over three weeks old in the wild, four weeks in a domestic situation) were likely to approach a human after weaning and only those rabbits that had been exposed to a cat when young did not fear the cat when older. Rabbit kittens that had not been handled or exposed to a cat avoided both after weaning.

To maintain the socialization started by the breeder, a young rabbit should have short daily sessions of handling and grooming in its new home. In addition there should be a gradual introduction to the normal stimuli present in your home or garden once your rabbit has settled in. If your rabbit will be living in your house, this process of exposure is often hectic by the very nature of our homes, as well as appliances such as washing machines and vacuum cleaners. The rabbit must be given an indoor cage or enclosed area that he can retreat to if necessary and should not be housed in a busy area of the home.

If you have taken on an older rabbit, handling and socializing may have been done in the rabbit's previous home, in which case it is still important to maintain regular contact and grooming whilst gradually exposing the rabbit to everyday occurrences. If the rabbit is already quite fearful then there is a lot of work to be done (see below) and there is no guarantee that the rabbit will ever be totally confident as early experience has such a huge impact on the behaviour of the adult.

Behaviour problems

Sometimes a rabbit appears to have a behaviour problem when really the owner is just misinterpreting their rabbit's natural behaviour. The list at the start of this chapter should help determine if the problem is natural behaviour occurring in an abnormal situation or an actual problem.

Outlined below are the most common behaviour problems that owners have with rabbits and some solutions. The advice given here is just a guide to the main causes and treatments for the most common problems.

Fear of the owner/environment

When a rabbit hasn't been well handled as a youngster, it is quite normal for that animal to be fearful of humans throughout its life. This may lead it to display aggression to prevent contact (see below) or it may lead to a rabbit that displays fear by running away, hiding and avoiding all forms of interaction.

As a prey animal, it is not always in a rabbit's best interest to make too much noise when it is scared (as this will draw attention to itself) so they do not whimper as a dog may. Instead they will flatten their body to make themselves as small as possible and will stiffen their body. Where possible they will run and try to hide although this is not always possible and may lead to the fear being displayed as aggression.

Treatment

These rabbits take a lot of hard, slow work to turn around, but many of the techniques outlined below for a rabbit that is aggressive when it is handled are appropriate.

The rabbit should be approached at its own level and time should be spent associating food with interactions with the owner. Although quite distasteful, it often helps to roll your hands in some dirty bedding before you interact with a rabbit with this sort of temperament – for a species that relies heavily on olfactory communication, smelling 'friendly' should help.

Prevention

Understanding how a rabbit exhibits fear through its body language can help prevent homing a rabbit that is naturally fearful, i.e. not taking home the rabbit that is crouching at the back of the hutch. When buying a young rabbit, look for a breeder who is rearing the rabbits within a busy environment and handling them regularly – this has been shown to prevent rabbits becoming fearful of their environment and us.

When the rabbit first comes home, keep them quiet and allow them to accustom themselves to their new home before trying to pick them up. Also ensure that you approach the rabbit, and pick them up, in a manner that will make them feel secure. There are sections on handling within this book (see Chapter 06).

Aggression towards owner

Rabbits can be aggressive towards their owners for a variety of reasons – the most common being fear. Fear aggression in an adult rabbit can develop through a lack of handling as a young rabbit or as a result of a bad experience during handling.

Each time the rabbit is handled, the rabbit feels nervous and eventually uses aggression – in the form of bites, scratches and kicks – to prevent being picked up. The behaviour then becomes learned as the rabbit discovers that it works.

Some forms of aggression occur over, what the rabbit would consider to be, territorial disputes. Typically the rabbit is aggressive each time the owner tries to feed the rabbit or clean out the cage. The rabbit's aggression can be quite severe and will be understandably off-putting to the owner who may consider re-homing the rabbit or having it put to sleep.

Treatment

If the rabbit is displaying aggression due to a lack of handling when young or a negative experience, it is important to stop

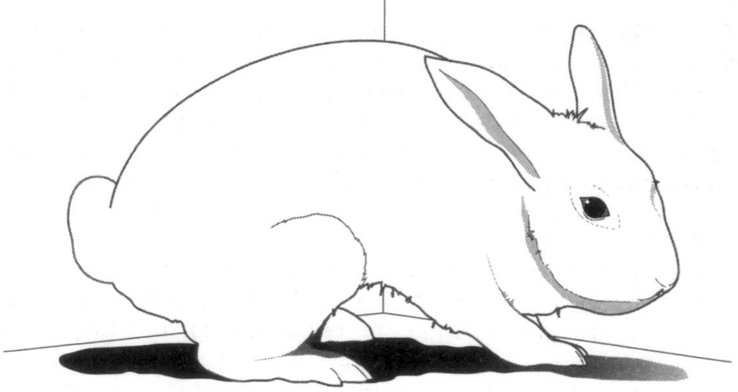

figure 13 a rabbit in depressive posture, this may lead to aggression.

attempting to pick up the rabbit for a period of at least six weeks. This time can then be used to teach the rabbit to alter the way it views the owner and gain confidence in interactions.

Initially, help should be sought to ensure that a correct method of handling was being attempted in the past. The original breeder of the rabbit or a vet may be helpful and if there are any problems they should be rectified by practising on another rabbit or even a life-sized cuddly toy!

The programme for teaching a rabbit to accept being picked up is as follows (and should be introduced for several short periods each day during the six week break):

- The rabbit's favourite treat should be identified and offered to the rabbit with no attempt to pick it up or stroke it. Hands should be rolled in some of the rabbit's dirty bedding first to remove any unusual smells.
- Once the rabbit is happily taking the treat (this may take a few days) gradually start to introduce small amounts of stroking. For very aggressive rabbits use a long-handled soft brush (that should be rolled in some of the rabbit's bedding first). If the rabbit bites the brush, keep it still so that the rabbit learns that aggression does not lead to the interactions stopping, and continue once the rabbit has calmed down and is eating the treat again.
- The use of the long-handled brush can be withdrawn by progressing to a shorter handle, and then holding the hand over the main head of the brush before finally removing the brush altogether.
- The next stage aims to introduce some of the more invasive components of handling one by one, whilst the rabbit is eating. They include laying a hand over the rabbit's shoulders, placing a hand lightly on the rabbit's rump and leaning over the rabbit.
- Picking up the rabbit only happens once the rabbit is totally confident in all of the above stages and may take a few weeks. At this point, sitting so that your lap is at the same height as the floor of the rabbit's home will help you to scoop the rabbit onto your lap where hand-feeding can continue.
- Finally, short periods of lifing can be introduced, always ending in a reward.

When a rabbit is territorially aggressive, it is worth having that individual neutered – particularly if the arrival of the behaviour seems to coincide with puberty (between four and six months of age). Providing more than one food bowl and lots of hay should dilute the rabbit's defence of what it perceives to be one valuable food area. Giving the rabbit a much larger and more challenging environment should also help to reduce the aggression.

Rabbits should not be punished for aggression as this will make them worse and will ruin the relationship between rabbit and owner. In situations where the rabbit is routinely shouted at or hit, the aggression worsens as the rabbit becomes increasingly defensive. Similarly, offering the rabbit something more appropriate to bite (such as a large gardening glove or a bar of soap) in the hope that this will put off the rabbit rarely solves the problem as it is addressing the symptom (the biting) rather than the cause (perhaps fear).

Prevention

As a prey animal, some rabbits have a tendency to view their owner as a threat; it is up to the owner to act as anything but. We often bend over rabbits, approach them suddenly or make lots of noise when we are around them – it is no wonder that they can become scared of us! Bear this in mind and approach from a different height – this will make a lot of difference to a rabbit's interest in being stroked or handled.

A good start in life with a breeder that has handled the rabbits from an early age can make all the difference and should prevent many problems associated with aggression.

Aggression towards another rabbit

There are rabbits who are aggressive towards other rabbits and this is something that we have to accept when we provide our rabbits with an enclosed area such as a hutch or run. The aggression can happen through fear – perhaps a rabbit that, for whatever reason, was not reared with other rabbits and displays nervous aggression when it meets a rabbit for the 'first' time.

More commonly, disputes between rabbits are caused by competition over resources. Same-sex rabbits can display aggression as they reach puberty (between four and six months of age) or during the breeding season.

Introducing a new rabbit to an existing rabbit may cause problems as they try to share the same territory and quite naturally compete over access to areas and resources – such as food.

Occasionally rabbits that have lived together quite happily can show aggression towards each other if they are separated and taken to the vet. Taking them to the vets together can prevent this happening. If rabbits that have lived together quite happily start to fight for no obvious reason then it is advisable to have them checked by a vet, as there may be an underlying medical condition behind the problem.

In some situations, rabbits may direct the fear of a situation into aggression towards a companion. An example of this may be if they have been scared by a loud noise or the presence of a predator.

Treatment

Neutering can help with some situations, particularly in the case of same-sex individuals that are fighting around puberty or at a certain time of the year.

A total revamp of the environment to make it larger and more complex, with more to do and areas that allow the rabbits to avoid contact with each other helps reduce aggression markedly. Introducing lots of hay and spreading out food between more than one food bowl should help reduce possessiveness and give them plenty to do.

When introducing rabbits to each other, simply putting a rabbit into an enclosure and 'letting them get on with it' often causes huge problems. Invariably the damage in some rabbit relationships is done during this first meeting and it can be very hard to ever re-introduce some individuals. The programme below for introducing rabbits on the first occasion can also be used for individuals that have fallen out of love.

- A neutral environment should be used for introduction; ideally this should be an area where the animals have not been before, such as a garden shed or the bathroom. Pick an area that has lots of furniture or fittings that could provide shelter or hiding places.
- Bring the rabbits together using small animal travel baskets, preferably the ones that allow the animal to look out the front and the sides. Feed the rabbits, with favourite treats, by hand through the sides of the baskets to teach them to associate the nice reward with the presence of the other rabbit.
- If the rabbits are not distressed or aggressive in the baskets, reduce the distance between the rabbits on a little and often basis over a period of several days. Keep up the treats and increase the distance between them if either individual reacts adversely.

- Assuming that the rabbits appear relaxed, the next time they come together can be without the baskets. Before this happens, another look should be taken at the room or place where this is going to happen to ensure that there are lots of hiding places and nothing dangerous. Placing lots of hay, green vegetables and healthy treats around the area will give them plenty to do.
- If this meeting takes place successfully then it should be repeated several times until the rabbits show relaxed behaviour or grooming towards each other. The rabbits should be separated at the end of each session.
- The rabbits can finally be introduced to their new home, which should be large with lots of feeding areas and places to hide.

Prevention

When obtaining littermates or a companion rabbit for an existing rabbit, an individual that is of the opposite sex makes for a more likely union. As soon as the rabbits reach puberty, one or both should be neutered to prevent pregnancy and behavioural problems developing.

When introducing a new rabbit, time should be taken to introduce them gradually and avoid throwing them together. A buck should never be put into a doe's hutch; to do so will cause enormous problems and probably quite severe injuries (this is also important for breeding).

The rabbits' hutch or home environment should be large and provide lots of boltholes and areas that allow the rabbits to avoid contact from time to time. Providing a healthy diet that allows the rabbits to perform natural eating behaviour and spreads the food throughout the territory can prevent some competitive problems developing.

Loss of toilet training

A perfectly trained house-rabbit can start to deposit faeces and urine in locations other than the tray as he or she reaches puberty. At this time, owners will describe how their rabbit runs in circles around their legs, possibly grunting and depositing faeces. On occasion a spray of urine may follow this. Sometimes rabbits will lose toilet training if there has been a sudden change in brand of litter or if the tray has become aversive for some reason (such as moving the tray).

Once a primary problem has developed, a secondary problem of over-marking can occur. In other words, if a rabbit stops toileting in the right place and starts leaving urine and faeces in the wrong place, any residual smells will encourage the rabbit to keep going in that area.

Treatment

Neutering is an effective means of reducing any toileting problems that seem to be associated with marking during puberty or at a particular time of the year (such as during the breeding season).

If toileting problems developed after a change of litter or location of the tray, then the litter and tray should be reverted to normal. If the rabbit is feeling threatened whilst it is using the tray – perhaps by another pet – then a tray should be put within an indoor hutch or other secure area.

Once an incorrect association has been formed (for example, the rabbit is routinely urinating on the sofa) it can be a very hard habit to break. One option is to confine the rabbit to its indoor cage with its food, water, toys and tray again for at least three to four days to reintroduce the toilet training.

Whilst this is being implemented, the areas targeted with urine or faeces must be thoroughly cleaned. It is a common misconception that products that remove the smell of urine to humans have the same effect on the animal responsible. Not so! Products containing ammonia (for example bleach) can encourage the rabbit to over-mark the area. Disinfectants and floral odour removers simply mask the smell to our inferior sense of smell.

A clean with a warm solution of a biological washing powder or using an enzymatic cleaner obtained through your vet should ensure that the area is clean enough to allow the rabbit supervised access in the future.

Any mishaps with urine should always be cleaned in the above manner, but if the problem is quite severe then access to certain areas may have to be denied for long periods of time to truly break the habit.

Whenever slip-ups occur, whether in toilet training, during puberty or for an undetermined reason later in life, punishment is not the answer.

Excessive chewing/destructive behaviour

The main reason for chewing or destruction is usually boredom. Rabbits naturally spend long periods of time grazing but as pets we give them a bowl of food that takes very little time to consume and not enough hay – consequently there is a large need to chew as this helps to wear their teeth down and keep their digestion running smoothly.

Treatment

There are many ways that the time spent eating can be increased, the easiest being to feed the rabbit mostly hay with a small amount of pellets or mix and some green vegetables. By feeding the rabbit a more natural diet we not only prevent health problems but we also reduce destructive behaviour.

There are also ways that we can encourage our rabbits to work a bit harder for their food; these include hiding the food or hanging it up high using hayracks or creating 'kebabs' on covered wire that can hang from the roof of the run or the doors of the hutch, making sure that any sharp ends are on the outside of the enclosure.

The rabbit's environment can also be re-designed to include items appropriate for a rabbit to chew – these include fruit tree branches, cardboard tubes or boxes. The provision of toys and areas to investigate also helps reduce problem behaviours.

When a rabbit lives alone, some company can help to relieve the boredom. Similarly a rabbit that lives in a hutch outside might benefit from coming into the home and living in an indoor cage.

Neutering is not generally advised as a treatment for this problem, although it can be helpful for females that are digging.

Prevention

Providing a natural diet, even in the home where it may be messy, can prevent many problems associated with boredom.

Before rabbits are brought into homes the area must be 'bunny proofed' to prevent any damage. The rabbit should then be given access to a large, safe area that includes toys and areas to investigate. Toys can be alternated and the environment can be changed around to provide as much novelty and stimulation as possible. For more information on bunny-proofing and enriching a rabbit's environment, turn to Chapter 06.

Neutering and behavioural problems

Neutering – spaying does and castrating bucks – does not help with every behavioural problem. However, it can be of use with those behaviours that are motivated by the sexual hormones, such as territorial aggression towards owners or companions and marking behaviours, such as spraying urine. It is a vital operation when mixing opposite sex rabbits to prevent a population explosion!

There are serious long-term health considerations for not neutering a doe that is not being used for breeding and most veterinary surgeons will advise on castrating a buck to prevent anti-social behaviours developing.

There are, of course, times when a rabbit has developed a behaviour problem and owners are at a loss and need professional help. If you are concerned by your rabbit's behaviour have them checked by your vet for any pain, discomfort or health problems and then seek professional help (see 'Taking it further' section at the end of this book).

08 genetics, reproduction and breeding

In this chapter you will learn:

- **how rabbits breed**
- **how to create your own strain**
- **how to hand rear orphans.**

Some people are interested in breeding their animals whilst many people are happy to have their animals as pets and replace them with new animals as and when something happens to them. Occasionally a rabbit comes along that you want to breed from when previously you have not been interested. Before you start breeding your rabbits, consider one thing – as we have seen in previous chapters there are many rabbits looking for homes in rescue centres. How can you guarantee that your rabbit's offspring are not going to end up there? The decision to start breeding rabbits should not be taken lightly.

Why do you want to breed your rabbits?

There are many reasons that people have for breeding rabbits; some of the main ones are:

- To let my family pet have just one litter because it is a natural thing for rabbits to do and seems healthier for my female.
- Because I have started showing and want to produce my own strain of a particular breed.
- I plan to produce animals for a third party, such as a pet shop.
- My rabbits got out together and my female is pregnant by accident.

It is worth pointing out that there is not much money in the pet rabbit market which, along with the concerns over the animals' health and welfare, suggests that trying to sell rabbits to increase your income may be naive. There are, of course, breeders that supply large numbers of rabbits to the pet trade but they are very large-scale producers and often provide other species as well.

Your local pet shop might be interested in the consequences of your 'one-off' or accidental mating but they have probably been offered many unwanted litters so may not be able to sell them for you. Your best bet, in this situation, is not to have the litter in the first place, but if all else fails advertise them to your friends and family as well as through your veterinary practice and then neuter your rabbits.

If you are breeding rabbits for the pet trade, make sure that you are handling the rabbits little and often from three weeks to ensure that they are not scared of people or normal environmental sights and sounds. Rabbits that have not been handled well at this young age are likely to develop behaviour problems associated with fear which may lead to them being put up for rehoming or put to sleep. This was obviously not your intention when you bred your rabbits but remember that once you home a rabbit you have little control over its future. If you want to have an effect on its prospects then ensure that your youngsters are well handled and confident when they leave your premises and that you spend time with the prospective owners, teaching them how to handle the rabbits, what to feed them and how they should live. The more time you spend on this, the more likely it is that your rabbits will stay away from the over-burdened rescue centres.

If you are breeding for exhibition purposes you should decide on the breed and colour that you are interested in. For this you may need to travel to rabbit shows to see all the different types and colours available whilst getting to know fellow breeders (for more information see Chapter 09). It is also helpful to decide how many rabbits you can keep and look after well, which is not necessarily the same thing. You will also have to consider what you are going to do with the rabbits that you do not want to keep.

What do you hope to achieve?

If you have decided to breed rabbits to produce your own strain of a particular breed, your first step is to have a firm idea of what you want to achieve. Ideally, breeding a top winner at a show would be nice, but how are you going to get that winning rabbit from the one on offer from the breeder?

All the rabbit breeds recognized by the British Rabbit Council are given a Standard which describes the ideal visual characteristics, weight, colouring and coat quality. Each of these qualities are allocated a maximum number of points (it varies from breed to breed) coming to a total of 100. The Standard helps judges make the right decision on the judging table. It is really important that you understand the Standard for your chosen breed, along with the faults, before you start breeding (for more information on your chosen breed, contact the British Rabbit Council or ARBA – details in the 'Taking it further' section at the back of this book).

Obtaining stock

Quite understandably, a breeder is unlikely to sell you his or her top rabbit. If you are lucky he or she may sell you a doe that has been mated by a winning buck, but generally you will purchase rabbits that are middle of the range animals and that are (hopefully) carrying the genetic material necessary for you to breed rabbits that are close to the Standard. A useful start is a trio of two does and a buck from one colour or strain that you are interested in (make sure you have some spare hutches ready for the offspring).

A good breeder should be able to advise as to whether the new rabbit would be successful on a judge's table, but it is also important to gain as much information as possible from national organisations, specialist clubs, websites and journals as well as spending time at shows watching the judging and noting the successful rabbit breeders.

The right breeder for you may not be the person that is doing all the winning – life isn't always that simple! As a beginner, you need a breeder that is helpful and has time for you. Of equal importance is the health and welfare of his or her stock so you need to see them in their own environment as well as on the show table. If the person you have contacted is not keen on inviting you to see his or her stock and is not being particularly helpful then they are probably not the best person for you.

A quick look at genetics

For thousands of years, man has used his knowledge of genetics to produce improved varieties of domestic animals and crops. It is only over the last hundred years or so that we have understood the process of heredity – the passing of genetic material from parent to offspring as discrete units known as genes.

Gregor Mendel, an Austrian born monk, is credited with the major work on inheritance, which he began in 1856. Mendel's first law (also known as the Principle of Segregation) states, 'the characteristics of an organism are determined by internal factors [genes] which occur in pairs. Only one of a pair of such factors can be represented in a single gamete [sperm or egg]'.

Put simply, every cell in a rabbit's body contains 22 pairs of chromosomes. Each chromosome contains lots of smaller units called genes that carry the information relating to characteristics such as size, coat colour, ear length, etc. Sperm contain 22 chromosomes whilst eggs also contain 22 chromosomes. When an egg is fertilized it contains 22 pairs of chromosomes and as the cell divides and increases in size, each created cell contains the same amount of information.

Genes carry information that is seen in the individual but they also carry information that relates to characteristics that may not develop. Genes are labelled as dominant or recessive depending on whether the appearance of the characteristic is suppressed or not. To keep everything simple, a dominant gene is labelled with a capital letter (*B*) whilst a recessive gene is denoted with a lower case letter (*b*). A rabbit could be carrying a gene that is *BB* (in which the characteristics of *B* would be expressed), *Bb* (showing the characteristics of *B*) or *bb* (showing the characteristics of *b*).

The genes that dictate coat colour are usually used to explain inheritance and the principles of genetics in animals and most authors use the genes for Agouti coat colour to illustrate the principles in rabbits.

The Agouti pattern of the wild rabbit's coat is produced by a gene, *A*. This gene mutated at some stage to produce a non-Agouti coat (known as the 'Self Black' – Self being used to describe a coat that is one colour all over). This mutant gene is denoted by *a*. A pure bred rabbit with the Agouti coat will carry the *A* gene in both chromosomes (*AA*), whilst a rabbit with a black coat carries both recessive genes (*aa*). Breeding an *AA* rabbit with an *aa* rabbit leads to offspring (called the F_1 generation) that all have the Agouti appearance but are *Aa* as the Agouti gene is dominant to the recessive black coat. This is known as a monohybrid cross.

Contrasting traits can be inherited together, such as colour and pigmentations, known as dihybrid (or two gene) inheritance. Mendel's second law (also known as the Principle of Independent Assortment) states that 'any one of a pair of characteristics may combine with either one of another pair'.

Mutations

Genetic mutations are caused by an alteration in the amount or structure of the DNA of the individual, which causes a change in the trait (genotype) that may be inherited. Mutations occur randomly and spontaneously and lead to the sudden appearance of a new characteristic – the coat of the Rex rabbits and the drooping of the ears which probably arose as a genetic mutation. The individuals that carry the mutation are then only bred with other individuals that appear with the same (or similar) feature to improve the trait.

Determination of sex

In mammals, each ovum (egg) contains an *X* chromosome whilst the sperm are split into those that carry an *X* chromosome and the other half that contain a *Y* chromosome. A male rabbit, for example, will have the genotype *XY* whilst a female will be *XX*.

The sex of the offspring of a mating is determined by which sperm fertilizes the egg. Random fertilization means that the gametes *X* and *X* from the female and *X* and *Y* from the male combine to produce *XX* or *XY* individuals in a ratio of one female to one male (in other words there is a 50 per cent chance that each offspring will be male or female).

Inbreeding

Inbreeding is the mating of related individuals to each other. Breeders may use this technique to improve a certain characteristic or feature. Close inbreeding – mating brother to sister, son to mother or father to daughter – is not recommended over several generations as it is likely that abnormalities will develop as well as a reduction in fertility. Mating individuals that have one parent the same is considered to be only moderate inbreeding, whilst mating half brothers and sisters together, but not every mating, is considered to be weak inbreeding. Many breeders try to improve their strains with a moderate form of inbreeding.

Line breeding

Line breeding is selective inbreeding that improves certain characteristics or qualities within a strain. Usually a group or a single rabbit is used as the head of the stud and mates with all the individuals of the opposite sex.

Outcrossing

Selectively mating rabbits with individuals that are not related to the strain is termed as outcrossing. This technique is often used to try and improve a characteristic but is not always straightforward due to the chance that the individual is not purebred and may be carrying a recessive gene for another factor that appears in the offspring as a fault.

Hybrid vigour

Hybrid vigour (or heterosis) is said to have occurred when an individual has been bred by crossing two unrelated individuals from other inbred lines. The resulting offspring (F_1) has better qualities than both parents.

The effect of the environment

The rabbit's environment can have an effect on some inherited characteristics. Light, temperature, water, nutrients and husbandry can all influence the development and growth of animals. For example, the size of the adult rabbit may be determined by diet, housing and health whilst the amount of offspring that a doe has may be determined by nutrients and husbandry.

Glossary of genetic terms

Allele: alternative forms of the same gene responsible for determining contrasting traits (represented as *B* or *b*).

Chromosome: a slender body in the cell nucleus that carries the genes in a straight line.

Dihybrid inheritance: the inheritance of two pairs of contrasted characteristics.

Diploid: an organism or cell having two sets of chromosomes or twice the haploid number.

Dominant: the allele which influences the appearance of the phenotype when present in the homozygous or heterozygous condition (represented as *B*).

F_1 generation: the offspring produced by crossing two parents.

F_2 generation: the offspring produced by crossing two F_1 individuals.

Gamete: a reproductive cell having the haploid number of chromosomes, especially a mature sperm or egg capable of fusing with a gamete of the opposite sex to produce a fertilized egg.

Gene: the basic unit of inheritance for a given characteristic.

Genotype: the genetic expression of a characteristic (represented as *BB*, *Bb* or *bb*).

Haploid: an organism or cell having only one complete set of chromosomes.

Heterozygous: the diploid condition where different alleles are present (represented as *Bb*).

Homozygous: the diploid condition where both alleles are identical (represented as *BB* or *bb*).

Hybrid: the product of mixing different species or varieties of animals or plants.

Locus: the position of an allele on a chromosome.

Monohybrid inheritance: the inheritance of a single characteristic.

Mutation: any event that changes genetic structure or any alteration in the inherited nucleic acid sequence of the genotype of an organism.

Phenotype: the physical expression of a characteristic, such as coat colour.

Polygenic inheritance: the appearance of a characteristic caused by the inheritance of a special gene complex (i.e. more than one gene).

Pure bred: an individual, or individuals, that produce offspring with the same characteristics generation after generation.

Recessive: the allele which only influences the appearance of the phenotype when present in the homozygous condition (represented as *a*).

Strain: a group of related individual bearing some resemblance to each other.

Test cross: crossing an individual of unknown genotype with a homozygous recessive individual to determine the exact genotype based on the offspring.

Traits: another term for characteristics such as coat colour or type.

Keeping records

It is important to keep records of matings to give you a greater understanding of your strain enabling you to use the principles of inheritance to improve certain traits. Records of matings can be kept using a computer programme (such as iBreed) or a log book and in the long term will enable you to provide valuable pedigrees to prospective purchasers.

Reproduction and breeding

In the wild, rabbits are usually sexually active at around four months of age. Our domestic rabbits vary but are usually ready to mate when the male is about four months old and the female is five months, although the larger breeds may be later than this, often around nine or twelve months old. The main breeding season in the wild is from late January until July/August so it would seem logical to start domestic breeding at this time to improve the success of the pregnancy. Many breeders try to breed all year round, particularly if they are hoping to have rabbits ready in time for a big show at a particular time of the year, but some rabbits will only breed when they are ready.

The phrase 'Preparation = Success' applies to breeding rabbits. A few months spent preparing will reap the benefits of a successful mating, a healthy pregnancy and vigorous young. To ensure that your litter have the best start in life, and bearing in the mind the effect that the environment can have on inherited characteristics (see previous section), breeding should start once your male and female rabbit are in perfect physical condition. Breeding from individuals that have a good coat but are inactive, aggressive, weak or unwell is short-sighted and will lead to problems, if not in the first generation then certainly in the future. Breeding rabbits that look beautiful but have a bad temperament may affect your chances on the show table as well as impacting on anyone that has one of your rabbits as a pet.

As with humans, fertility can be improved with a good diet, regular exercise, space and mental wellbeing. Many breeders recommend the introduction of Vitamin E into the diet (in the form of wheatgerm) for its effect on fertility although rabbits are unlikely to suffer from a Vitamin E deficiency if they are fed a well-balanced diet. If your doe is overweight, reduce her weight using the tips in Chapter 04.

The male

The male's sperm are contained within the two testicles that are located within the scrotum, found at the base of the rabbit's stomach, in the crook of the hind legs. In the wild rabbit, the testicles withdraw into the abdomen outside the breeding season, descending the following year. It is also thought that the testicles are withdrawn during hierarchical disputes between males. The sperm pass into the female through the penis, following mating and ejaculation.

The male rabbit, or stud buck, is the most important rabbit in the breeder's shed and breeders will often have more than one fit and healthy individual who carries all the sought after traits of the strain.

The female

The female rabbit produces eggs from the ovaries, which travel towards the womb and implant in the wall of the uterus once they have been fertilized by sperm. Like domestic cats, ferrets and camels, rabbits have an unusual system of ovulation called reflex (or induced) ovulation that means they ovulate in response to copulation rather than on a cycle, or season. The signal for ovulation is sent from nerves supplying the reproductive organs and lower half of the body to the hypothalamus in the brain. The hypothalamus signals the pituitary gland to release lutenizing hormone (LH) that will cause the follicles to erupt releasing the egg.

Female rabbits produce pre-ovulatory follicles (follicles contain eggs) that last for about a week and without mating will degenerate whilst a set of replacement follicles mature. Once a successful mating has occurred, the fertilized eggs will become embryos that will imbed into the wall of the uterus and gain their own blood and oxygen supply by the development of the placenta.

In the wild or in domestic colonies of rabbits, the buck may mate the doe from day 14 of her pregnancy onwards so that she is pregnant almost immediately after giving birth to the initial litter. In this way, rabbits are able to have up to six litters in an average breeding season (although this is not advisable in a domestic situation).

The basics

Rabbit courtship is quite quick and simple; it has undoubtedly evolved this way to enable the males to have sufficient time to mate another female. The male follows the female and then circles her with a stiff-legged gait that also raises the tail and is called 'tail-flagging'. An interested female will lie by the male and flick her tail in response to his parades whereas a disinterested female will ignore the attention and may even wander off.

Mating takes place when the male positions himself on top of the female, often holding her neck with his teeth. The act itself is very quick and the male usually falls off the female, perhaps making a sharp noise like a scream. Once the male has recovered himself, the buck and doe return to previous activities, such as feeding.

In the domestic situation, breeding is of course more controlled – the buck and doe can be put together in a run or other enclosed area or the doe can be placed in the buck's hutch. Never place the buck in the doe's hutch – mating will be the last thing on her mind and she may injure the male as she defends her territory.

How to tell if a doe is pregnant

The gestation period of the rabbit is approximately 31 days. During this time the rabbit shows very few outward signs until about halfway through when she will start to increase in size. Experienced breeders may be able to feel the litter at this time by running their hand under the rabbit's body, just above the sexual organs, where it is said that the developing rabbits will feel like small balls. Another method is to consider the rabbit's mammary glands, which should feel swollen and thicker during the third week of the pregnancy.

A few days before giving birth, the doe will start to prepare a nest using bedding from the hutch as well as hair from her chest. Once the doe has prepared her nest she should be left alone but given ad lib access to food and water. A doe that prepares a nest around day 16 of the pregnancy may be having a phantom pregnancy (see below and Chapter 10) that would indicate that she is not pregnant.

Ideally the doe's hutch should be cleaned out for the last time pre-birth before she starts to make her nest but if you miss the chance, you can use a tasty treat to keep her in the nest half of the hutch whilst the rest of the bedding is removed and replaced.

Many breeders introduce nesting boxes into the hutch at this time so that the doe has a chance to leave her young in an enclosed environment. This gives a more natural approach to parental care, enabling the doe to visit her babies once every twenty hours, as she would in the wild. Of course, once the babies are big enough to climb out of the nest box it will not save her from their interest.

Phantom pregnancies and other problems

Some rabbits develop the symptoms of pregnancy when fertilization has not taken place. This is called a phantom (or pseudo) pregnancy and is caused by the hormones that were produced as the eggs were released. The rabbit will appear swollen, make a nest and may produce milk from the mammary glands. Usually the condition will end 16 to 18 days after mating when the bodies that are stimulating the reproductive system degenerate. After a phantom pregnancy, the doe is hyper-fertile and a mating at this time is likely to be more successful than the last.

Fertility problems can occur in bucks and does. Often they are a consequence of a health issue, such as poor diet, but may also occur if a rabbit has had a break from matings – perhaps due to a long show season or changes in the breeder's commitments – but is often amended once regular mating is reintroduced. As with all animals, there are some individuals that seem to be incompatible with each other although successful with others, whereas some rabbits may not breed during the colder months and wait until the start of the warmer weather and lighter evenings.

Any obvious issues with fertility should be reduced in your strain by not breeding with these individuals. Breeding rabbits that exhibit high fertility and good parenting skills will make your strain more successful.

The doe and her young

Young rabbits are borne naked, blind and dependent upon their mother for food. The mother feeds them milk from her mammary glands every twenty hours or so and spends the rest of the time eating, drinking and being quite inactive. Most litters are born during the hours of darkness, presumably as a defence against predators in the wild rabbit. It is not advisable to check the rabbits too often but it is useful to ensure that all is well quite early on.

To do this, separate your doe – who will probably welcome the break – either into a separate hutch or contain her in part of her own hutch and distract her with a nice treat, such as a cabbage leaf or a small piece of carrot. Roll your hands in some of her dirty bedding to disguise your smell and then gently part the bedding of the nest to expose the young. If there are any stillborn young remove them, otherwise count up the babies (an average litter size is six) and replace the bedding. Return the doe to her hutch and resist the temptation to look again until the babies start to move around when they are a little older.

The milk that rabbits produce to feed their young is very rich in protein and high in energy to enable the young to develop quickly. As a consequence a doe will require lots of food whilst she is lactating as well as freedom to drink plenty of water – it is wise to replenish both twice a day so that she does not go without. (For further information on feeding lactating does see Chapter 04.)

From three weeks, the young will start to leave the nest and investigate the hutch and some of the mother's food.

Problems with the doe and her young

Sometimes, you will visit your doe and litter but find that the young have died or that a baby has been pushed out of the nest. On some occasions, the doe may appear to have eaten all or part of her young, and at other times the babies may have been scattered around the hutch, nowhere near the nest.

As heartbreaking as these finds are, the priority is to save any young that have not died whilst removing the dead. Remember to roll your hands in some dirty bedding before you do any handling and temporarily remove the doe to another hutch in case she becomes protective over her territory or the remaining litter. Young that have been scattered from the nest but are still alive can be warmed in the hand and then returned to the nest and covered over with the bedding.

Does often leave their young or cannibalize them if they feel that the environment is unsafe or if the mother is not healthy – raising a litter uses a huge amount of the mother's energy and it will not be expended if she does not consider them to have much chance of survival later on. There are some pregnancies that end in the womb, for much the same reasons, and the foetuses degenerate and dissolve before being resorbed.

If the doe is not interested in her young or is not able to feed the youngsters then fostering or hand-rearing is an option (see section later in this chapter). Youngsters that leave the nest before three weeks may do so if the mother is short on milk – the doe should be checked for any problems and her food and water intake considered and increased if necessary.

First-time mothers may have problems with their litter but does that have had several litters can suddenly appear to lose all maternal instincts. The important thing is to be conscious of the individual's health before, during and after pregnancy and to provide a quiet and secure environment in which to give birth and raise their young.

Sexing young rabbits

Sexing rabbits correctly is vital to prevent unwanted early pregnancies. Sexing adult rabbits is not that difficult but it is worth knowing how to compare the two by looking at the physical differences between adult rabbits before trying to decipher the much smaller sexual organs of a young rabbit (for more information and diagrams see Chapter 03).

Weaning

In the wild, the mother weans the kittens when they are about 24 days old, but in the domestic situation the young are usually weaned later, at around four weeks, at which point they are consuming greater quantities of solid food and less milk. The reduced need leads to the mother producing less milk until her body stops altogether. (For further information on feeding youngsters see Chapter 04.)

When to separate

Once the doe has weaned the youngsters and her milk has dried up, she can be removed to a new hutch leaving her litter to manage without her. Although this seems harsh, young rabbits in the wild are left by the mother at just over three weeks so although the youngsters have a period of adjustment to her absence they will usually settle down within a few days.

Some young rabbits can start to become sexually active whilst still with their litter mates – whilst a mating at this time is unlikely to lead to a successful fertilization, any mounting behaviour is a sign to separate the rabbits and decide what to do with them. If you are keeping the offspring for breeding they can be removed to new hutches, whereas the rabbits that are going to pet homes can be kept in same sex groups for a little longer. It is worth remembering, however, that rabbits have a tendency to compete with each other over resources in a limited space, particularly with the onset of puberty.

Selecting the rabbits to keep

If you are breeding a marked breed for showing, this decision will be straightforward as the markings will be apparent on most breeds from a young age. Similarly the coat quality of some rabbits is apparent by five or six weeks old. Each breed has particular faults that an experienced breeder will be able to pinpoint, either in the nest or once the kittens have emerged, and then decide whether to breed from that rabbit, keep it for exhibiting purposes or offer it as a pet.

For the novice breeder, this is not so easy and there is plenty to be learned by trial and error. A deciding factor on who to keep is often space and there is not always room for sentimental decisions.

Leg rings

Rabbits that are to be shown need to wear a ring around the hind leg that carries a serial number linking each rabbit to its owner. Leg rings are purchased from the British Rabbit Council and are sized according to breed. In the US and some parts of Europe, rabbits are identified by a permanent tattoo in their ear. When a rabbit is sold, a transfer card must be completed so that the new owner is able to show the rabbit; to do otherwise will break the rules of the governing body.

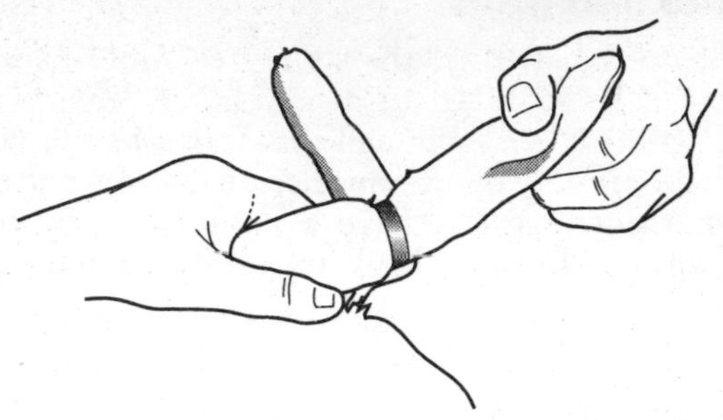

figure 14 identification ring on hind leg

Leg rings are placed over the foot of most breeds of young rabbits when they are around eight weeks of age; the ring sits above the hock joint. Although the rabbit's leg will thicken and widen with age, this should not cause the ring to tighten and will prevent discomfort later in life (although the ring should still be checked regularly).

Fostering rabbits

If rabbits are neglected by the mother or for some reason the mother is unable to feed them, then you may have to consider fostering or hand-rearing. If you have a doe available who is feeding another litter then you may be able to introduce some individuals to her nest for her to foster. This can only take place prior to three weeks of age but is more likely to be successful if the rabbit is under ten days old. The young should be introduced to the nest whilst the doe is absent or occupied and she should be encouraged to stay away from the young for as long as possible to enable the foster kittens to smell similar to the rest of the litter. Obviously the doe should be watched, at a distance, to check that she does not behave adversely towards them.

Hand-rearing rabbits

From time to time, rabbits may stop feeding their young due to illness or poor maternal skills, but be sure they have actually been abandoned before you start hand-rearing. Remember – female rabbits only feed their young once in a 20- to 24-hour period. If the babies have been scattered around the nest and the mother has milk then it is worth warming the kittens in your hands and then putting them back in the nest. If they are scattered again a few hours later or seem to be dehydrated, then hand-rearing may be the only option.

The following information on hand-rearing has been included courtesy of Mairwen Guard of Cottontails Rabbit and Guinea Pig Rescue (for contact details, see 'Taking it further').

You will need:

- milk formula
- milk substitute (Cimicat, Lactol or Esbilac)
- Avipro (probiotic) or similar – usually available from your veterinary practice
- Abidec multivitamin drops – available from chemist/ supermarkets
- a box (high-sided or with lid, allowing for passage of air and daylight) lined with a towel/shavings with hay on top, placed in a warm area (important for newborns). This will need to be swapped for a larger more suitable cage as the babies grow and become more active, such as a plastic indoor cage sold in most pet shops. If the mother managed to pull fur to line the nest, then it is a good idea to use this to help keep newborn babies warm. Change the bedding daily or as required. You will also need another smaller box for use during the feeding routine (see below).

There are two main ways to foster feed:

- By syringe – use a 1ml syringe for rabbits under three weeks old, or a 2ml syringe for rabbits over three weeks old (both available from your veterinary practice). The larger size is much more difficult to use so feeding may be more successful if 1ml syringes are used throughout.
- By 'bottle' – using a foster feeding set (Catac Products) and extra teats.

Preparation of Milk Substitute

1 part milk substitute: 2.5 parts cooled boiled water. Add 1/4–1/2 teaspoon probiotic and 0.5–1ml multivitamin drops depending on the quantity of milk prepared. Enough milk should be prepared each time to allow for one day's feeds, keeping it in the fridge between feeds. Syringes, teats and other feeding equipment can be left soaking in a fresh solution of sterilizing fluids between feeds, rinsing thoroughly before use.

Establishing a feeding regime

It is vital that newborn babies are kept reasonably warm until their fur has grown sufficiently (this is usually when they are around seven days old). This is especially important for single orphans, although care must be taken not to let them overheat – babies must always have the option of crawling away from the heat source if they need to.

The younger the baby is, the more difficult it is to hand-rear successfully. Firstly, it is very difficult to control the amount of milk going into the rabbit's mouth at a time, and if care is not taken it will breathe milk into its lungs (usually confirmed by milk coming out of the nose) resulting in aspiration pneumonia which is usually fatal. This should not be confused with the accidental intake of milk up the nose, which does not usually cause any major damage. Secondly, baby rabbits need their mother's milk not only as a source of nourishment but also to supply them with the appropriate gut bacteria for them to be able to digest their food (milk) properly. Without this they fail to thrive, develop diarrhoea and die. This is the reason why probiotics are added to the milk substitute with every feed. It is common for hand-reared rabbits to grow into adults that have an intolerance of diet change and may be sensitive to too many green vegetables.

Although the mother rabbit only feeds her babies once a day, the milk being fed during hand-rearing is not as rich as the 'real thing' so the orphans need to be fed three or four times a day, spacing the feeding times as evenly as possible. It is not necessary to feed during the night unless they are not feeding well, in which case feed them every few hours until they are taking a few millilitres at a time. The quantity of milk taken varies from infant to infant and from one feed to another. The guide below is gives an indication of how much you can expect a baby rabbit to take on a daily basis.

A baby rabbit of one day old would consume on average 2ml of milk daily. By five days the volume would increase to about 12ml. At ten days it would increase again to about 15ml, by 15 days to 22ml, 20 days to about 27ml, 25 days to about 30ml. By 30 days of age you would expect to see a decline to about 20ml, and by 35 days a rapid decline to less than 5ml or weaned altogether.

Baby rabbits can take two to three days before they settle into a feeding pattern, and if there are several to be hand-reared it is beneficial to feed all babies once, placing each one in the smaller box after feeding as you go along to ensure that you don't miss anyone, and then go round again to make sure they have all had enough to last until the next feed. It is common for a kitten who has only taken a small amount at the first sitting to be very greedy at the next. Again, replace the babies one at a time into their home cage when they have had their second feed. They should have the appearance of looking content and full, the milk in the stomach being visible through the skin in very young babies. The appearance of nice round, full bellies should not, however, be confused with bloat, an extremely serious condition which is caused by the gut becoming static and with a resulting build-up of gases. A rabbit with bloat will not feed normally, and in the latter stages will not eat or drink at all. Immediate assistance from an experienced vet is essential, but sadly this condition is often fatal (for more information see Chapter 10).

The milk should be warm but not hot (test it by putting a few drops on the back of your hand). Hold the infant with one hand whilst gently inserting the teat or syringe into the mouth with the other. Baby rabbits often wriggle around and jump whilst feeding so take care not to drop them! If the babies are under 6 days old you will need to stimulate urination. This is a straightforward task. After each baby has been fed, wet a finger or cotton bud in warm water and gently tap or stroke the genital area. Have a tissue ready!

By about three weeks of age the babies will start to nibble on hay, followed shortly afterwards by small amounts of rabbit food. Use a good brand of pellet food. At this point you will need to introduce a water bottle at a suitable height so they can reach it, enabling them to drink whenever they want to. If you find you have one or two babies still enjoying the milk routine after four and a half weeks, gradually wean them off over a period of a week.

It is recommended not to give hand-reared babies any fresh fruit or vegetables until they are at least four months old, and even then to introduce it very gradually. The only exception to this rule is if hand-rearing wild rabbits, as in these circumstances it is vital that they are offered a wide variety of grasses and other plants that they would normally find in the wild from about three weeks onwards. With domestic rabbits, stick rigidly to one type of good quality dried food, and if there has to be a change at any stage, mix the two foods together for at least a couple of weeks, gradually increasing the new variety until the change over has been made. Very little (if any) dried food should be offered to baby wild rabbits as it will aid their release into the wild if they are given as natural a diet as possible.

Post-weaning care

As mentioned earlier, hand-reared baby rabbits are more prone to digestive upsets than mother-reared babies, and it is vitally important to stick rigidly to one type of feed, and not to introduce fresh food until at least four months of age (and only then with extreme caution). Post-weaning enteritis usually kills within hours, and appears to be brought on by a change of pH (change of acidity/alkalinity) in the gut resulting in the overgrowth of hostile bacteria such as *Clostridia* and *E. coli* which replace the natural friendly bacteria. Absorption and digestion is affected, resulting in bloat and/or diarrhoea, dehydration and death. Stress can also play an important part in triggering post-weaning enteritis, so care must be taken to keep this to a minimum, especially if the rabbit is re-homed before four months of age.

09 exhibiting rabbits

In this chapter you will learn:

- **how to prepare for a show**
- **how to enter a show**
- **how to understand showing terms.**

Many people find rabbit breeding and showing to be a competitive and rewarding hobby as well as a chance to make new friends and speak to experts who know all the tips and tricks of successful rabbit keeping. As with everything in life, there can be some setbacks – such as losing stock to illness or failing to do well at shows – however these are all minor compared to the sense of achievement when your rabbit wins its class or is even awarded a Best in Show.

The rabbit fancy

The collective term for a group of enthusiasts who follow a specific pursuit or breed an animal for particular qualities is a fancy. The people that breed their rabbits, usually to exhibit them at shows, are called fanciers.

The first exhibition rabbit was the English Lop which was created in England and initially exhibited in 1840. As new breeds were introduced, and specialist breed clubs started, there was a need to have a central body responsible for recognizing the new breeds and to cater for members.

The British Rabbit Council is the governing body of the UK rabbit fancy (ARBA is its American counterpart) and was formed in 1934 to license shows, regulate conduct at shows, protect and further the interests of its members and to present a unified voice to government, or other interested parties.

The breeds recognized by the British Rabbit Council are classified as Fancy, Lop, Fur or Rex rabbits and each breed is given a Standard which is an outline of the ideal for breeders to try and create in their strain and for judges to use when comparing the rabbits in a class (see below).

Rabbit Clubs

The British Rabbit Council has many national and area specialist clubs as well as local rabbit clubs dotted across the country. In addition, agricultural societies that hold rabbit shows at their annual events are affiliated. ARBA have National Speciality Clubs as well as Chartered Clubs (such as Regional Speciality or local).

In the UK, there is only one National Specialist Club for each breed and in 2006 there were 48 clubs (there are more recognized breeds than national clubs as some breeds are combined together, for example the National French & Dwarf Lop Club). Each national club has a panel of judges who are elected by the membership. They will usually hold two shows a year – an Adult Stock Show and a Young Stock Show.

An Area Specialist Club is similar to the national club but is restricted by its area, the East Anglian Lop Circle for example. In 2006 there were 78 and each one of them represented a particular breed or similar breeds. Each area club is affiliated to the British Rabbit Council and approved by the national club.

Local clubs provide a network of fanciers from a small area who are interested in a variety of breeds but are passionate about rabbits. Local clubs provide a chance to regularly meet up with people who have similar interests and often hold seminars and get-togethers alongside regular shows. In 2006 there were 101 local clubs in the UK and just under 400 in the US. Membership of your local club and National Club is recommended.

British Rabbit Council shows

The British Rabbit Council supports shows for its members by offering awards and granting a star status – from the basic one-star show to the two-day, five-star showcase events. The overall aim of the show is to recognize the rabbits that are closest to the Standard and worthy of championship status.

Each show is advertised in *Fur & Feather* magazine and outlines the time, date and venue of the show along with the judges, prize money and awards as well as a list of classes. There are many classes at each show listed under the headings Fancy, Lops, Fur or Rex. Exhibitors must stipulate which classes they are entering when they submit their show entry (for more information on entering shows, see below) by looking for their breed and then its colour. If the colour is not listed, then the rabbit maybe entered in the Any Other Colour (AOC) or Any Other Variety (AOV) section.

The first section of judging is the classes and the judge will look at all the rabbits entered in that class, for example all the White Angoras. He may disqualify some rabbits at this stage (see below) and award the first, second and third placing out of the remaining rabbits. This will be done with adults and the under-five-months rabbits will be judged in the same way. Finally the best adult rabbit will be judged against the best under-five-month rabbit to award the Challenge Certificate for that breed.

Once the classes are over, the judge will move onto the Section Challenges – at most shows these are under-five-months (u/5), adult (Ad) and any age (AA) so the judge will bring out the rabbits that he thinks are up to standard and worthy of competing against others in the same section. This is often quite confusing as it is not always as straightforward as the rabbits that won their class – the rabbits entered into the Section Challenge are there at the judge's discretion.

Three-, four- and five-star shows offer duplicate classes, where winners from the breed classes, categories of exhibitor or rabbit compete against each other. Entry in these is optional to the exhibitor. To decide the Best in Show rabbit, the judge uses the equivalent of a duplicate class called a Grand Challenge. The judge considers the adults and u/5 rabbits that have won their section – Best Fancy, Lop, Fur and Rex. He will then pick the best adult and u/5 rabbit overall before deciding which rabbit is the better of these two and Best in Show.

The three awards offered by the British Rabbit Council are:

- **Challenge Certificates (CCs):** these are offered by the British Rabbit Council and are awarded to the adult or under-five-months rabbit in each class if the judge considers the rabbit to be worthy of championship status. The winners of the CCs then compete for the title of Best Fancy, Lop, Fur and Rex who are then judged to award the Best in Show. A rabbit is considered a champion once it has won a certain number of CCs, under a minimum number of different judges, as detailed by the British Rabbit Council and the National Specialist club. A CC won at a four-star show is considered to be worth four points, whereas a CC awarded at a one-star show is only one point.
- **Best of Breed certificates (BoBs):** these are awarded to the rabbit considered to be the best of its breed when the breed has several colour varieties. The judge will compare all the rabbits of the same breed that have won CCs before awarding this certificate. BoBs can only be awarded if the show is holding more than two classes for that breed.
- A diploma is awarded to the winner of the Section Challenges and the Best Fancy, Lop, Fur and Rex rabbit (if there are sufficient sections). Diplomas always count as one star when adding them to CCs for championship status.

Each club will offer varying amounts of prize money and rosettes as well as particular trophies – for example, Best Junior or a memorial trophy to accompany a Best of Breed award.

Star status is awarded by the British Rabbit Council and carries certain conditions which are as follows:

- A one-star show is often a small affair held over one day. The British Rabbit Council stipulates that a one-star show must offer 15 CCs with at least one in each section of Fancy, Fur, Lop and Rex. Prize money is optional and these shows are an ideal starting point for new judges or exhibitors.
- A two-star show is similar to a one-star show but offers a minimum of 25 CCs with at least one in each section of Fancy, Fur, Lop and Rex. Two-star shows are held regularly all over the country on most weekends of the year and provide a venue for the newcomer to see many different breeds of rabbit and to meet breeders.
- A three-star show is usually a one-day National Specialist Club stock show or an All Breed Championship and must offer prize money. (Please note that this applies to British Rabbit Council Shows, not ARBA.) Three-star shows offer a minimum of 45 CCs with at least ten in each section and at least one separate duplicate class for Fancy, Lop, Fur and Rex.
- A four-star show is a one-day championship show held in a large venue and offering a minimum of 55 CCs with at least 15 in each section and at least one separate duplicate class for Fancy, Lop, Fur and Rex. Prize money for classes may not rise above that offered for a three-star show but a four-star CC, BoB or Diploma, due to the greater level of competition, is prestigious. Four-star shows are open for the public to attend and require a veterinary surgeon to be available.
- There are only two five-star shows in the country, one is held in the London area and the other in Yorkshire. The Excel London Championship Show is held towards the end of the year (usually in early September) whilst the Bradford Excel Small Livestock Show is held in January. These shows are the showcase events for the British Rabbit Council as they not only attract many exhibitors but also members of the public. Both events are held over two days and offer a minimum of 70 CCs with at least twenty in each section and at least one separate duplicate class for Fancy, Lop, Fur and Rex. A veterinary surgeon is in attendance and a full show catalogue is issued at a five-star show. A Best in Show at a five-star show is the pinnacle of accomplishment in the rabbit fancy but even a five star CC, BoB or Diploma is considered an immense achievement. Attending one of these events is a must for any newcomer to the rabbit fancy.

Breed shows

If the show is being held by a breed club, for example the National Miniature Lop Club, then you can only enter Miniature Lop rabbits at that show. National Specialist and Area Specialist clubs often hold shows in conjunction with other clubs where they are said to be 'being entertained' by the other club. For example, the South Western Area Dutch Rabbit Club may hold a show at the West Hants & East Dorset Fanciers show. The host club will have classes for the breed that is having a specialist show so exhibitors enter their rabbit into both shows. A four- or five-star show will usually entertain many specialist clubs.

Junior Certificate of Merit shows

Juniors (over five and under sixteen years of age) are encouraged within the rabbit fancy. A Junior Certificate of Merit (COM) show offers a special award for the winning rabbits in each class, but these awards are not CCs and cannot count towards Championships. Juniors can enter their rabbits in the main show as well as the Junior COM and their rabbits are judged against the Standard.

Box shows

Box shows rarely have a star status awarded by the British Rabbit Council. Although they are unable to award CCs and they do not have to offer any prize money they are very popular local events. Box shows provide a less competitive environment for the newcomer to see what the judge thinks of their rabbit.

Pet Shows

Many clubs offer a pet show alongside their star show. Pet shows are seen as lots of fun but also encourage newcomers to the fancy. The rabbits do not have to have any identification (ring or tattoo) and the owner does not have to be a member of a governing body. The judge will award the rabbit that is clean, healthy and has a good temperament, and the club may offer rosettes and trophies. Awards include Boy's Pet, Girl's Pet and Adult's Pet.

Entering a show

The first time you enter a show can be quite nervewracking. You may find that a kind member of the rabbit fancy will enter your rabbit on your behalf, but if not, the secretary will be able to help you, as long as you provide the following information:

- the breed and colour of the rabbit
- the age and sex of the rabbit
- whether or not you bred the rabbit.

Some shows offer a Block Entry Fee that means that you pay one fee, which covers all the classes that your rabbit is eligible for. If the show does not offer this then you choose the classes that you want your rabbit to enter and pay for each. Lucky Pen classes are a bit of fun and if you pay the fee for every rabbit that you have entered then you may win a lump sum at the end of the show when the pen numbers are drawn out. The British Rabbit Council adds a levy to each exhibitor (it is as low as 25p) but it is one amount per exhibitor, not per rabbit. Some clubs incorporate this amount into the entry fee. Juniors may have to pay no entry fee to enter the COM if they have paid to enter a class in the main show. Entry into the pet show is usually offered at a reduced fee.

Once you have worked out the classes that your rabbit is eligible for based on breed, colour, sex and age then move onto the Duplicate, or Grand Challenge, classes. It is not sensible to miss these classes out as you should give your rabbit the chance to be brought out for the judge at any stage throughout the show. A rabbit cannot be entered in any class if it has not been entered in a breed class.

The show adverts listed in *Fur & Feather* magazine include the secretaries details, how they can be contacted and, most importantly, the date that entries close. This is usually a few days before the show itself but the larger shows will close earlier to enable them to prepare the paperwork in time for the show.

Preparing for a show

The preparation of a really good show rabbit happens long before the show date with the fancier keeping the rabbit in good health, with a good diet and regular health checks and handling. Other than cleaning and tidying there is not much that can be achieved on the morning of the show itself!

When rabbits are judged, they are placed on a table and the judge handles each rabbit in turn. The rabbits that do well are usually the rabbits that meet all the requirements of the class and sit well – rabbits that lie flat on the table and struggle when they are handled may not do so well, even if they are close to the Standard.

It is important that your rabbit is handled regularly and trained to pose when it is placed on a table. From a practical point of view, this involves a few minutes each day but can be rewarding for both you and the rabbit. Young rabbits that are handled regularly are known to be less likely to display fearful behaviours when they are older and can make very successful show rabbits, assuming that they are physically healthy and close to the Standard.

Grooming should be a regular part of your routine, and should not be left until the morning of the show! In the breeds that have longer hair, knots are most likely to occur between the back legs of the buck and dead hair can often get overlooked on the dewlap of the doe (for more information on grooming see Chapter 06). A problem for breeds with longer hair or white hair is staining on the feet – this should be checked for and removed prior to the show using a dry shampoo or a chalk powder that can be brushed out. In the week prior to the show, rabbits with white feet should be cleaned out regularly as it is often urine that causes the staining, although running around on the lawn is probably not sensible either.

There are, of course, some things that can be done in the run up to the show. Rabbits can have a final groom and their nails should be checked to ensure that they are not long. Also check around their back ends to ensure that there are no faeces stuck in the fur, particularly on the morning of the show itself.

The practical preparations for the show should be done the night before the show, particularly if you have an early start in the morning. A good checklist is as follows:

- Write the ring number of each rabbit that you intend to show on a piece of paper and put it somewhere safe so that it will be to hand when you arrive at the show.
- Find any car passes, entry tickets or booking-in cards that the show secretary has sent you and plan your route to the show. Try to arrive at least 45 minutes before judging starts to give you a chance to find your bearings and settle your rabbit.
- Work out your clothes and don't wear anything that you don't mind being covered in rabbit hair and general mess. Many fanciers wear white coats to protect their clothes (for stockists, see 'Taking it further').

- Prepare the travel box to ensure that it is not dirty inside and will keep your rabbit clean. Place some clean bedding such as fresh shavings or an absorbent product (such as VetBed) in the base of the box. Beware of newspaper that might mark your rabbit with ink, or using straw, which is not very absorbent.
- Pack some shavings and straw for the pen (a carrier bag full should be sufficient), a water bottle and a way of attaching it to the pen, some bottled water, some hay and some greens or another treat to keep the rabbit occupied once judging has finished. If you are worried about your rabbit being bored in the pen all day then a willow ball stuffed with hay or a favourite toy is acceptable.
- Put together a grooming kit that comprises a comb, some nail clippers, kitchen paper, cotton wool and a brush.
- If the weather is warm, plan to leave in the cooler part of the day and a bit earlier so that you have time to stop and check on the rabbits.
- If you are driving to the show, tidy and prepare the car the night before so that there is plenty of room for the box or boxes.

It is acceptable to give a rabbit a quick check over before you place them in their pen, but if you have been preparing them for several weeks before you should not need to give them a full groom as soon as you arrive at the show. Although you will see people doing it, it is not really considered acceptable.

Arrival and booking in

If the secretary has sent you your pen number and booking-in cards already, you can put your rabbit into the pen and then join the queue at the secretary's table to book in. Fill in the ring (or tattoo) numbers on one half of the card and hand it to the secretary. If the secretary has not sent you these details then you will be given the card to complete and the pen number when you book in (make sure that you have your ring numbers to hand when you join the queue). You must book in a pet rabbit and if you have brought fewer rabbits than you originally entered, let the secretary know which rabbit is absent.

If you have not paid your entry fee already, then you will be asked to pay once you are booked in.

The pen provided by the show should contain some shavings already but not enough to provide a thick cover so add your shavings and attach the water bottle. Put the hay into the pen but leave any pellets or vegetable matter until after the show, just in case they cause any staining. Place your rabbit in the pen and go and get yourself a refreshment!

Once judging starts, you are free to watch, have a drink or chat to fellow fanciers. Some fanciers help the judging process by stewarding, which is a great way to learn more about the judging. Most clubs are pleased for the offer of help so let the secretary know if you are interested.

The judge and the steward

The judge's decision is final because they have trained for the position and have been asked by the show organizers to give their opinion on the rabbits at the show. Some judges are 'all rounders' having proved their knowledge across the range, whereas others specialize in breeds or collective groups. For example, a judge might be termed a Fancy Judge as he knows a lot about fancy rabbits or he may be highly sought after for Polish rabbit shows, as this is his speciality.

Judging usually takes place on long trestle tables covered with a white sheet. The judge and the book steward are positioned on one side whilst the stewards on the other side of the table line up the rabbits. The stewards go backwards and forwards between the table and the pens collecting and returning rabbits as the judge goes through the classes. When a rabbit is brought to the table, the book steward hands a small sticky label to the steward and this is placed insider the ear or on the nape of the rabbit's neck. The label bears the pen number of the rabbit and keeps any other details about the rabbit anonymous to the judge. When your rabbit is being judged, it is not wise to make any noise or action that might alert the judge to the rabbit's ownership – this is not good showmanship nor is it acceptable etiquette.

The judge considers each rabbit in terms of the standard. Each breed has a Standard, which is a set of recommendations for the physical appearance, weight and feel of the rabbit. Each of the factors, including coat colour, ear length, weight and length of the rabbit are allocated a certain number of points enabling the judge to mark the exhibit. The Standard provides breeders and judges with an ideal specimen, which then prevents too much variation within the physical characteristics of the breed.

example of a breed standard (British Rabbit Council)

Netherland Dwarf

		points
1)	body	30
2)	ears	15
3)	head	15
4)	eyes	5
5)	colour	15
6)	coat	10
7)	condition	10
	Total	**100**

The book steward holds a very responsible position, as it is their job to aid the judge. Book stewards also manage the stewards by reading out the pen numbers of the rabbits that the judge wants to see on the table and preparing the ear labels. In addition, they fill in the judging sheets with the details of the winners and placings, the details for the CCs and BoBs and generally help the judge to finish on time with no hold-ups.

After the show, the judge writes a report on the winning rabbits that is published in *Fur & Feather* magazine along with photos of the winning rabbits or the exhibitors. In the US, reports and news are published in *Domestic Rabbits Magazine* which is sent to members of ARBA.

Disqualifications

Rabbits may be disqualified from the show if they exhibit any signs of ill health, malocclusion, nails the wrong colour for the breed or if the rabbit is overweight (the ideal weight is outlined in the Standard). In addition, there are some breeds that have specific disqualifications, such as a white spot on the nose of an English rabbit (called a 'putty nose') or white patches of hair within the main body colour of a Rex.

Once the judging is over

Even though the judging of your rabbit may take only a couple of hours, rabbits cannot be removed from the show until all the judging has been completed. Once the Best in Show has been announced (usually on a stage), the secretary or treasurer will be ready to pay the prize money to the winners. Prize money can only be claimed on production of the retained half of the booking-in card and any prize cards that were put on the rabbit's pen. If you don't claim your money at the end of the show it will usually be considered as a donation to the club.

Once the pens are empty, the show volunteers start to clear up – they are always grateful for the help so if you have a few minutes, help take down some pens or sweep the floor.

When you return home, put your rabbit back into his hutch or indoor cage with plenty of hay, some pellets and water and leave him to recover from what has probably been quite a long day.

British Rabbit Council guide to showing terms

AA – Any Age.

Adult – A rabbit of breeding age or above the age stated for young classes.

AC – Any Colour.

Ad – Adult.

All Rounder — Applied to persons who are recognized as experts on all varieties, as opposed to Specialists, who are experts in a number of breeds.

Amalgamation — The joining together of two or more clubs or (in the case of shows) of two or more classes.

AOC – Any Other Colour.

AOV – Any Other Variety.

ASS – Adult Stock Show.

AV – Any Variety.

Awards – Any card awarded to a rabbit at a show.

B or B – Black or Blue.

Breeder – The owner of the mother of a rabbit at the time of its birth.

Breeder Class – A class confined to exhibits bred by the exhibitor.

Breeding Doe – A doe of breeding age.

Cards – Award cards are issued to successful exhibits at shows. These are generally for special prizes, first, second, third, fourth, Reserve (R), Very Highly Commended (VHC), Highly Commended (HC), Commended (C).

Challenge Certificates – Certificates awarded at Star Shows by the BRC to rabbits of outstanding merit owned and registered in the name of individual members of the BRC.

Challenge Class – A class open to all or confined to a special type of variety or rabbit such as Fancy, Lop, Fur or Rex breeds.

Champion – An animal that has won a championship, awarded by the BRC.

Chest – The front of a rabbit, running from the chin down to the forelegs.

Chopped-off Rump – Instead of being nicely rounded, the rump is more or less at right angles to the back.

Club Judges – Judges elected by Specialist Clubs as qualified to judge special breeds, whose awards will be recognized for club championship and special prizes.

Cobby – A type desired in certain breeds such as Dutch rabbits (the opposite to racy).

Dewlap – A pouch of skin under the neck of certain breeds, usually only found in does.

Diplomas – Offered by the British Rabbit Council for the best exhibit at Open Shows which may either be penned or table events.

Double Champion – A rabbit which has qualified for a second championship certificate.

Duplicate Classes – Classes in which a rabbit may be entered additionally to its ordinary breed class (Challenge, Novice, Breeders, etc.).

Duplication – The entry of a rabbit into several classes at one show.

Ear Label – A small gummed label which is stuck in the ear of a rabbit at shows bearing its pen number.

Fancy Breeds – An arbitrary division of the breeds (which is by no means really accurate). These include Angoras, Belgian Hares, Dutch, English, Flemish Giants, Harlequin, Himalayans, Lops, Netherland Dwarfs, Polish, Silver and Tans.

Full Coat – The Adult coat with no signs of moult.

Fur Breed – The opposite to Fancy Breeds; often includes Rexes, Satins and then the Normal Fur Breeds such as Argente, Beveren, Californian, Chinchilla, Chinchilla Giganta, Fox, Lilac, Havana, New Zealand Red, New Zealand Black, New Zealand White, Sable, Siberian and Smoke Pearls.

Gentleman's Class – A class confined to exhibits owned by men (over 16).

Guaranteed Classes – A class in which full prize money is guaranteed regardless of the number of entries secured.

Heavy Breeds – One of the larger breeds such as Flemish Giants, Chinchilla Gigantas or Beverens.

Hock – The joint on the hind legs of a rabbit above the foot and below the shoulder.

Intermediate Stock Show – Caters for both young and adult stock.

Judges List –A list of Specialist Clubs and BRC approved judges published yearly by the BRC.

Junior Class – Confined to exhibitors over five and under sixteen years of age.

Lady's Class – A class confined to exhibits owned by women (over 16).

Limit Class – Confined to exhibits that have not won more than three first prizes in open competition.

Local Club – A club, the activities of which are confined to a limited area.

Local Show – Show unable to claim star grading.

Moult – The shedding of one coat and growth of new fur.

Moult Mark – A mark frequently shown between the old and new fur when a rabbit is moulting. Sometimes this lasts until the next complete moult, indicating the animal has only partially moulted.

Novice Exhibit Class – Exhibit not to have won a first prize at any show except in members' classes or at a Table Show.

Novice Exhibit and Exhibitor Class – Neither the owner nor the exhibit to have won a first prize at any show except in members' classes or at a Table Show.

Open Class – Class open to all except where confined to a breed or breeds or to a specified age group.

Pair Class – A class for two rabbits of the same variety, matched as closely as possible in size, colour, etc. The sex, unless especially stated in the schedule, is optional.

Pen – Wire cage used at shows for displaying the exhibits.

Pen Number – The number given to a rabbit at a show, which will appear on the address label sent to the exhibitor, on the show pen, and also in the catalogue and judging book.

Pen Show – Shows that provide pens for all exhibits.

Points – (a) The ears, tail, nose and below the hocks and joints of the forelegs in breeds such as the Himalayan; (b) a scale of points and drafted Standard showing the ideal to be aimed for in different breeds.

Putty nose – A white spot on the nose extremity.

Raciness – The type in Belgian Hares, approaching the wild hare.

Rex Fur – The type of coat found in the Rex varieties where all the guard hairs are shortened in length and thinner in diameter so that they can not be distinguished from the undercoat.

Ring – The most common method of marking and recording rabbits recognized by the British Rabbit Council.

Show (Open) – A show open to any exhibitor.

Show (Penned) – A show in which pens are provided for all exhibits.

Show (Specialist) – A show confined to limited and specified breeds.

Show (Table) – A show where pens are not provided for the exhibits, after being judged on the table the rabbit is replaced in its travelling box.

Specialist Breeder – A breeder who concentrates strictly on a variety.

Specialist Judge – A judge recognized as an expert in the variety concerned.

Standard – Description of the ideal to be aimed for in each variety as drawn up by the Specialist Club and BRC.

Star Scheme – A prize scheme based on the number of stars won by an individual animal.

Star Show – A pen show run under BRC rules for which Challenge Certificates and Diplomas have been granted by the BRC. These may be one-, two-, three-, four- and five-star shows.

Stewards – Officials appointed at shows to take charge of the exhibits and assist the judge.

Sweepstake Show – A show at which prize money is not fixed but varies from class to class according to the entries received.

Type – The appearance and conformation of a rabbit.

Young Fancier – Persons between the ages of 16 and 21 years inclusive who register with the British Rabbit Council.

Youngster – A rabbit under Adult Age.

YSS – Young Stock Show.

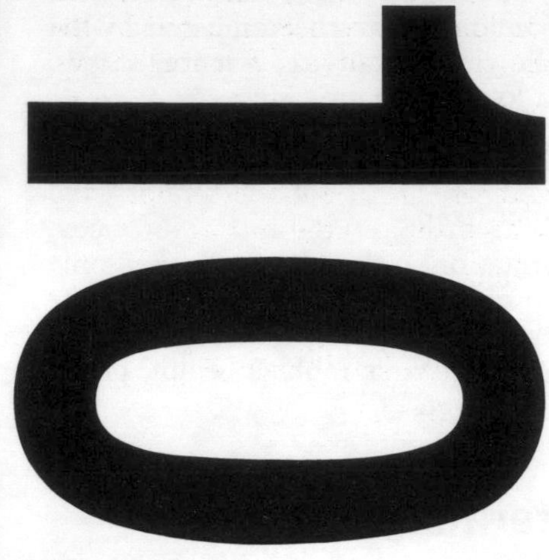

health care

In this chapter you will learn:

- **how to tell if your rabbit is in pain**
- **how to recognize common ailments**
- **how to look after an elderly rabbit**

In previous chapters of this book, you have learned how to house your rabbit, what to feed it on, how to handle it and what 'normal' behaviour is. By following this advice, you are likely to have a rabbit that will live a long and happy life.

However hard we try, problems do sometimes occur so this chapter aims to provide a brief overview of the illnesses and ailments that rabbits can suffer from.

It is important that the information in this chapter is used only as a guide to the range of problems and diseases that may be suffered by a rabbit. It is not intended for self-diagnosis; if you are concerned with any aspects of your rabbit's health, please make an appointment with your vet.

How to find a veterinary surgeon

Veterinary medicine for rabbits has come a long way over the last ten years and more and more vets are now offering extensive treatment for rabbit patients. However, there are still some practices without a resident 'expert' so it is up to you to find a practice that you are comfortable with.

Unless you have received a recommendation from a rabbit-owning friend, you will need to call or pop into a few local practices and ask some questions. Your telephone directory or the Royal College of Veterinary Surgeons website should help to point you in the right direction (www.findavet.org.uk) in the UK. The House Rabbit Society in the US (www.rabbit.org) have a recommended veterinarian list.

Asking if there is a vet in the practice with an interest in rabbits should pinpoint one or two individuals for you to consult. Inquiring about the price of vaccinations or neutering should also give you an idea of the level of interest. Some practices have designated areas just for cats and small animals to help minimize their stress. In addition, some surgeries offer regular rabbit health checks, new owner packs and even education nights for owners.

Be prepared to travel to the practice that is most likely to help you if you have an emergency.

Preventative measures

It is always easier, and less heartbreaking, to prevent or spot a problem early on.

We should inspect our rabbit daily to check that it is eating and drinking at a normal rate, is not behaving differently – such as appearing very tired or being suddenly aggressive – and does not have any faeces or staining in the anal area. If you feed your rabbit at the same time every day you will quickly notice if there has been a change in their eating or drinking habits. Make sure that any droppings appear normal and that the water bottle is being used.

Hutches and litter trays should be cleaned out every few days and in the warmer months this is one of the few ways to avoid attracting flies that may lay their eggs in your rabbit's hutch, or on the rabbit itself.

On a weekly basis, teeth, nails and ears should be checked and trimmed or cleaned if necessary. Running a hand over your rabbit's body will give you an idea of the condition of its skin and coat and also will give an indication of its weight. Body shape and sizes of rabbits vary so much but as a general rule, you should be able to feel your rabbit's spine and ribcage but the bones should have a covering of flesh. If you can feel your rabbit's spine 'jutting out' then you may need to increase the amount or quality of their diet. On the other hand, if your rabbit has a very deep covering of flesh, you may need to consider cutting back!

All rabbits can be vaccinated against the fatal diseases Myxomatosis and Viral Haemorrhagic Disease (VHD). These must be administered as advised by your vet and kept up to date.

How to tell if your rabbit is in pain

In the wild, an injured rabbit is easy prey for a predator so they have evolved a survival mechanism that means that if they are in pain, they rarely make a noise. In fact, if a rabbit screams with pain they are usually in excruciating agony or dying.

As owners we need to know how to understand the more subtle changes in our rabbit's behaviour to understand how they are feeling.

A rabbit that is in pain is usually quieter, moving around less and appearing to be very lethargic. They may be stretched out and floppy or sitting in a hunched position. Their behaviour could be described as 'depressed' meaning that their normal responses are reduced or lowered. When a rabbit is in lots of pain, it may grind its teeth.

What to do if you find a problem

The diagnosis and treatment of an injury or illness should always be performed by a vet. If a routine check alerts you of a problem, basic first aid can be administered by placing the rabbit in a cardboard box or travel cage with some bedding and then finding a quiet room of the house. Try to keep your rabbit quiet and warm and away from pets or children.

An appointment should be made with your vet as soon as possible. If your rabbit has a companion, it can minimize the stress if the animals are moved as a pair, unless either rabbit is in obvious distress.

A word of warning – waiting to see if your rabbit gets better of its own accord runs the risk that he or she will worsen to the extend that he or she is beyond help.

Listed below are some of the common ailments and diseases of rabbits. The problems have been grouped according to the area of the body with a section at the end for miscellaneous problems. Each ailment covers symptoms, possible cause, probable treatment and preventative measures.

Digestive problems

Constipation (gastric stasis)

Symptoms

The rabbit has stopped eating, there are no faeces in the rabbit's hutch or litter tray and its abdomen appears swollen. The rabbit may be showing signs of pain, such as grinding teeth. The rabbit may also be reluctant to move.

Cause

Constipation occurs when the movement within the digestive system comes to a halt. Pain and dehydration then cause the rabbit's general well-being to be affected. Feeding a diet low in fibre or too high in fat is often the reason.

Treatment

The rabbit must be taken to a vet promptly. Painkillers may be administered along with drugs to stimulate the gut and fluids to re-hydrate the rabbit.

Prevention

Rabbits should be fed large quantities of good quality hay on a daily basis with a pellet feed or mix (of at least 18 per cent fibre and less than 16 per cent protein) and some green vegetable leaves. Fresh water and regular exercise should be readily available. Sugary treats, fruit and non-green vegetables should be avoided.

Diarrhoea (enteritis)

Symptoms

The rabbit's faeces are brown and watery and there may be some mucus. Mucoid enteritis is a specific syndrome that affects rabbits just after weaning, when they are 7–14 weeks of age, and has a high mortality rate.

Cause

Diarrhoea can be caused by infections, a sudden diet change, a diet low in fibre, stress and following a course of certain antibiotics.

Treatment

The rabbit will need to be given fluids (orally or via a drip) by a vet and treatment to keep the gut bacteria levels normal. Removing the rabbit's mix and just feeding lots of hay and blackberry or raspberry leaves can improve mild cases. Specific antibiotics may be required, especially in young rabbits, in outbreaks of infectious diarrhoea.

Prevention

Rabbits should be fed large quantities of good quality hay on a daily basis with a pellet feed or mix (of at least 18 per cent fibre and less than 16 per cent protein) and some green vegetable leaves. Fresh water and regular exercise should be readily available. Sugary treats, fruit and non-green vegetables should be avoided. The addition of a probiotic supplement may be helpful.

Sticky bottom (excess caecotrophes)

Symptoms

The rabbit produces more of the sticky faeces than it consumes and they can become stuck in the fur around the anus.

Cause

Rabbits kept in confined spaces, overweight, elderly or arthritic individuals or those with teeth or spinal problems may not be able to reach around and consume the faeces. A diet low in fibre, high in protein and sugar may also be to blame.

Treatment

Initially the rabbit must be given unlimited access to good quality hay and pellet mixes or treats should be removed. A better quality pellet or mix should be introduced once the situation has improved. Overweight rabbits should be fed less and given more exercise. A vet will advise on tooth and spinal problems.

Prevention

The rabbit should be fed large quantities of good quality hay on a daily basis with a pellet feed or mix (of at least 18 per cent fibre and less than 16 per cent protein) and some green vegetable leaves. Fresh water should be readily available and the rabbit should have plenty of exercise. Sugary treats, fruit and non-green vegetables should be avoided.

Coccidiosis

Symptoms

The rabbit is not eating; it may appear bloated due to an enlarged liver and may have diarrhoea. This condition is often fatal.

Cause

The rabbit has become infected by the parasite *Eimeria* which affects the liver or the gut.

Treatment

The rabbit must be taken to a vet who will diagnose the problem and, if possible, administer treatment.

Prevention

Hutches should be cleaned regularly to prevent infections. Pellets containing a coccidiostat can be fed to control rather than cure infections of the gut but they are only recommended for large rabbitries where the chance of infection is greater.

Urinary problems

Red urine

Symptoms

Urine is discoloured. It is quite normal for rabbits to have urine that is sometimes an orange or brown-red colour.

Cause

A rabbit's urine can change colour after consuming large quantities of carrots, or when fed a mix with coloured ingredients. Rabbits that are dehydrated may produce darker urine. Blood in the urine is a serious sign that can be caused by several diseases.

Treatment

Ensure that no other health issues might be causing the rabbit to be dehydrated. A vet can test for blood in the urine and this must be investigated and treated if present.

Prevention

As red urine is usually normal there is little prevention needed although feeding a balanced diet and checking the rabbit regularly can prevent the development of problems.

Urinary stones (Urolithiasis)

Symptoms

The rabbit appears to strain during urination, loses all sense of 'litter training', may be lethargic and in pain. Blood may be present in the urine.

Cause

The build up of alkaline crystals, called 'stones' within the bladder or kidneys. Sometimes the stone may become lodged in the urethra. Diets high in protein and calcium increase the build-up of crystals. Stones are more common in overweight, inactive rabbits.

Treatment

A vet will x-ray the rabbit and administer fluids, painkillers and antibiotics. If the stone is large the rabbit may need to be operated on to remove it.

Prevention

A diet low in protein (less than 16 per cent) and calcium can prevent the build-up of stones. Feeding large quantities of hay and a small amount of pellet or mix can help as well as avoiding sugary treats. Keeping urine diluted by offering lots of fresh water and green vegetables is imperative.

Cystitis

Symptoms

The rabbit may appear to be in pain as it urinates and the urine may contain blood.

Cause

Inflammation of the bladder, caused by a bacterial infection.

Treatment

Once diagnosed, a vet will administer antibiotics. Vitamin C can help with healing.

Prevention

A recurrence of cystitis is quite common and this can be prevented by diluting the rabbit's water with unsweetened cranberry juice. Dandelions increase the flow of urine and can be helpful.

Respiratory problems

Snuffles (Pasteurella)

Symptoms

There are many symptoms including mucus from the nasal passages, pneumonia, conjunctivitis, an ear infection, breathing difficulties and abscesses on the womb, testicles or teeth.

Cause

Many rabbits can carry the bacterium *Paseturella multocida* for long periods before developing any symptoms or they may show no signs and pass the infection onto their offspring or other rabbits that then develop symptoms. *Pasteurella* can be passed by direct contact with other rabbits and is highly contagious. Other bacteria can cause similar signs.

Treatment

A prolonged course of antibiotics may reduce symptoms and get the situation under control, but rarely eradicates the infection altogether. The rabbit should be maintained on a healthy diet to boost the immune system.

Prevention

It is thought that stress, a poor diet and changes in husbandry can reduce the rabbit's immune system leading to the development of symptoms in a rabbit that was a carrier. Feeding a good quality diet, maintaining good hygiene and introducing change gradually may prevent outbreaks. Rabbit hutches should be regularly disinfected and owners should wash their hands each time they handle a rabbit. A new rabbit should be kept away from any existing animals for a period of two to three weeks in case symptoms develop.

Allergies

Symptoms

Sneezing, breathing difficulties.

Cause

Rabbits can develop allergies to wood shavings, cigarette smoke, perfume, pollen, dusty hay.

Treatment

Once the allergen has been identified, exposure of the rabbit to it can be reduced or prevented. Vets may prescribe antihistamines or steroids to reduce the symptoms in difficult cases.

Prevention

As the development of allergies is quite rare there is little preventative advice although it is sensible not to expose rabbits to cigarette smoke. Any changes in bedding or hay should be introduced gradually and regular checks allow problems to be identified quickly.

Teeth, eye and head problems

Overgrown or uneven teeth (malocclusion)

Symptoms

The rabbit is not eating or grooming itself and may be losing weight. Sometimes the rabbits overgroom themselves or a companion. The rabbit may also dribble excessively, develop watery eyes, and have soft faeces stuck to its bottom area. Overgrown front teeth (incisors) can usually be seen by opening the rabbit's mouth, and in some cases grow out of the mouth. Problems with the back teeth (molars) can be harder to see.

Cause

The rabbit's teeth are growing out of line and are not being worn evenly. In some rabbits this is an inherited problem or a consequence of skull shape, but in others it is a result of damage to the mouth or a poor diet.

Treatment

Teeth are gently reshaped by a vet using a dental burr. Incisors can be removed under anaesthetic.

Prevention

Rabbits should be eating a diet high in fibre and calcium. Access should be given to fresh grass or hay, green vegetable leaves or dandelion leaves, and pellets should be fed to rabbits that have a tendency to pick out the best bits of a complete mix. As Vitamin D is involved in the absorption of calcium, rabbits should have access to natural sunlight.

Head tilt (torticollis, or 'wry neck')

Symptoms

The rabbit carries its head on one side and may have lost all sense of balance.

Cause

Middle or inner ear infections are a very common cause. *Encephalitozoon cuniculi* produces spores that can migrate to the brain and kidneys. Head tilt may be a consequence of an infection with this parasite. Strokes, poisoning or an injury from a fall can could also affect the normal carriage of the head. Some rabbits develop a head tilt as a consequence of a *Pasteurella* infection.

Treatment

Diagnosis of the cause by a vet. The rabbit may require a course of treatment to reduce swelling and antibiotics.

Prevention

Regular health checks and confident handling to prevent injuries. Good hygiene can prevent infection with *E. cuniculi*.

Tear duct infection (dacrocystitis)

Symptoms

A thick white discharge from the eye and sometimes a discharge from the nostril on the same side of the head. The discharge can make the skin around the eye dry and sore.

Cause

Tooth disease or a bacterial infection (such as *Pasteurella* or *Staphylococcus*).

Treatment

A course of antibiotics administered by a vet and eye drops to take home. The tear duct may require flushing initially with sterile saline and an x-ray will ascertain the state of tooth roots.

Prevention

Feeding a good diet to prevent dental problems developing and practising good hygiene.

Skin problems

Fly strike (blowfly myiasis)

Symptoms

The rabbit will be damp and smelly around the back end with maggots seen around the anal opening and under the skin. The rabbit may appear to be lethargic. Rabbits are very likely to die from an infestation, or may need to be put to sleep by the vet.

Cause

Blowflies lay eggs on soiled skin and maggots hatch within 24 hours. Fly strike is often a consequence of poor hygiene but a rabbit with dental problems, sticky bottom or diarrhoea, or an overweight/elderly rabbit (who is unable to remove the faeces) can be at risk.

Treatment

If the rabbit is alive, the maggots have to be removed and in many cases the rabbit is treated for shock with fluids and painkillers. Antibiotics will also be given.

Prevention

Fly strike is very easy to prevent by regularly cleaning and disinfecting hutches, daily checks of the rabbit and feeding a high-fibre diet to maintain weight and reduce the likelihood of dental problems. If a rabbit is suffering from sticky bottom syndrome, or any other digestive disturbance, the cause should be identified and treated. Electric fly zappers, sticky papers and tea tree oil or lavender can be used outside the hutch to discourage flies.

Ear mites

Symptoms

The rabbit has itchy ears and a build-up of earwax. If left untreated the rabbit's ears will become inflamed and red with thick yellow crusts.

Cause

The mite *Psoroptes cuniculi* lives on rabbits and can often infect the ear. The mites can often be seen within the ear as they can grow to a length of 0.7mm.

Treatment

The ear mite wax/crust may need to be softened before it can be removed. Infested rabbits will be given an injection and the environment will be treated with a proprietary flea spray to prevent further infestations.

Prevention

Rabbits that the infected rabbit comes into contact with must be treated to prevent further infestations. Regular cleaning and disinfecting of hutches and litter trays can prevent problems, whilst regular checks can highlight problems before the ears become very inflamed.

Fleas

Symptoms

The rabbit may be seen itching excessively. If the coat is brushed whilst the rabbit is standing on a white surface – such as a sheet of paper – flea 'dirts' will be seen as small black dots.

Cause

Fleas breed very quickly passing from one host to another and quickly reach epidemic proportions. A possible carrier can be another animal within the home as rabbits can harbour not only the rabbit flea (*Spilopsyllus cuniculi*) but also the cat and dog fleas (*Ctenocephalides felis felis* and *Ctenocephalides canis*).

Treatment

Discuss with the vet the best topical treatment for your rabbit and treatment of the rabbit's environment to kill all eggs and avoid later re-infestations.

Prevention

As biting insects, such as fleas, pass myxomatosis it is really important that owners routinely check and treat their rabbit whilst discouraging flying insects from the hutch and rabbit.

Mange mites

Symptoms

The rabbit has patches of thick dandruff with fur loss. The condition does not appear to cause any irritation and the problem may coincide with the start of warmer weather. The condition can be passed to humans, leading to a rash.

Cause

The non-burrowing mite *Cheyletiella parasitovorax*.

Treatment

The rabbit may be given an injection and a bath to remove the mites and treat the skin infection. The hutch and bedding will need to be treated with an insecticide.

Prevention

Regular cleaning and disinfecting of hutches and litter trays may prevent infestation. Owners should wash their hands before and after handling each rabbit.

Ringworm

Symptoms

The rabbit has itchy sores, not necessarily shaped like rings, but reddened and hairless. The condition can be passed to humans.

Cause

Ringworm is a fungal infection caused by *Trichophyton mentagrophytes* or *Microsporum canis*. The infection can be passed from cats, guinea pigs or other rabbits with spores living for around 18 months.

Treatment

The hair around the sores may be clipped away and then treated with a shampoo or cream. The rabbit may be given an injection in severe cases. Any areas of the environment that the rabbit has been in contact with must be disinfected whilst other rabbits should be monitored.

Prevention

Ringworm can be prevented in the same way as Mange Mites (see p. 147).

Vent disease ('rabbit syphilis')

Symptoms

The rabbit has developed crusty sores on the genitals that may spread to the face. If untreated, the disease can lead to problems with fertility in both sexes.

Cause

The disease is caused by an organism called *Treponema cuniculi* and is passed from one individual to another at mating, during birth or when feeding the young.

Treatment

All affected rabbits and all those that are likely to come into contact with the infected rabbit, will be treated with penicillin. This is the only situation where rabbits are given penicillin, which is normally considered too dangerous to use.

Prevention

Rabbits with Vent disease should be treated as soon as the sores become apparent to prevent infecting other individuals.

Reproductive problems

Phantom pregnancy

Symptoms

The female rabbit may become territorial, have enlarged mammary glands and start pulling hair from her chest area to build a nest, but she is not pregnant.

Cause

An unsuccessful mating, mounting by another female, over-zealous stroking from an owner or exposure to a male rabbit may cause a doe to ovulate. As there is no sperm to fertilize the egg the rabbit exhibits a phantom pregnancy.

Treatment

This will last for around 18 days after which she should return to normal. If the owner intends to breed from the doe, she can be put with a stud buck as soon as the false pregnancy has passed.

Prevention

Mating a doe again within five hours of the original act should prevent an intended mating becoming an unsuccessful phantom pregnancy. A doe that is not required for breeding purposes and has had one or more phantom pregnancies should be neutered.

Cannibalism of young

Symptoms

Young rabbits (kittens) may be partially or totally consumed by the doe.

Cause

If the doe feels that the environment that she has given birth in is not safe, secure and appropriate she may consume her young rather than investing her energy and resources in their upbringing.

Treatment

There is nothing that can be done if the young are all dead.

Prevention

Ensure that a pregnant doe is kept in a quiet area, fed well and not disturbed (particularly during the last week of pregnancy and the first week after birth). She should be given fresh bedding, large quantities of water and a good diet. Ensure that the hutch is spacious and that other rabbits or pets are not allowed near her.

Womb cancer (*Uterine adenocarcinoma*)

Symptoms

Often seen by blood or blood clots in the urine – the rabbit must be taken to the vet immediately. Untreated the cancer can spread to the liver, lungs and to mammary tissue.

Cause

A cancerous growth developing on the womb or ovaries. Womb cancer is thought to affect up to 80 per cent of does over the age of four years and commonly develops in does from two years of age.

Treatment

Ovariohysterectomy (removal of the womb and ovaries) is successful if the cancer has not spread to other organs.

Prevention

Spay does, before they reach two years of age, if they are not to be used for breeding.

Mastitis

Symptoms

The rabbit's mammary glands will be hot and painful. The rabbit may be lethargic and not eating. The condition can occur in rabbits that have had a litter but can also occur with a phantom pregnancy.

Cause

Damaged nipples and teats that become infected as well as poor hygiene. In some cases mastitis can be fatal for the doe and her young.

Treatment

A vet will administer an antibiotic and painkillers. The young must be hand-reared to prevent infection of another doe if fostered.

Prevention

Good hygiene can help prevent the development of mastitis.

Viral diseases

Myxomatosis

Symptoms

Swellings develop around the eyelids, the genitals, the nose and the ears. The rabbit may develop a conjunctivitis which leads to blindness. The rabbit will eventually stop eating but its appetite may be unaffected initially. Rabbits usually die from a secondary infection such as pneumonia.

Cause

A pox virus introduced into the UK in the 1950s to control wild rabbit populations. The virus is spread from rabbit to rabbit by biting insects such as fleas or mosquitoes.

Treatment

The scale of the problem depends on the rabbit's immunity and is fatal in unvaccinated rabbits. If vaccinated rabbits develop the disease, the rabbit will probably survive following a course of antibiotics and careful nursing, but it may take a long time for the nodules to heal.

Prevention

Rabbits should be protected by a vaccination at least once every six months – whether living indoors or outdoors. The control of fleas and mosquitoes is also important.

VHD (Viral Haemorrhagic Disease)

Symptom

A dead rabbit or a sudden death sometimes following convulsions and nose bleeding. A rabbit may not have been eating and appeared quite lethargic prior to death.

Cause

VHD is a virus that is spread directly via rabbit nasal secretions or indirectly via other animals, contaminated feed or clothing. VHD causes haemorrhages within the main organs of the body.

Treatment

Not usually an option as the first sign that the rabbit had VHD is once it has died. A post-mortem can confirm the disease.

Prevention

Individuals can be protected by a vaccination every year as soon as they are over ten weeks old – whether living indoors or outdoors. Ensure that insects and other animals are kept away from the hutch. Good hygiene helps – cleaning the hutch with a disinfectant and changing clothes and washing hands after handling other rabbits.

Miscellaneous problems

Sore hocks (Pododermatitis)

Symptoms

The hocks of the back legs may be ulcerated or bleeding.

Cause

Friction with a hard surface, such as a cage floor or carpet. It is particularly common in breeds that do not have much hair on their hocks – such as Rexes. Overweight rabbits may also develop sore hocks, as there is greater pressure on their legs.

Treatment

The rabbits need to be kept on soft, clean bedding and the wounds can be treated with a healing cream, although full hair regrowth is dependent on age with older rabbits less likely to recover totally.

Prevention

Keep your rabbit's weight down, their nails short and ensure that they always have access to soft bedding. This condition may be inherited, so individuals with this problem should not be bred from.

Paralysis

Symptoms

Inability to move whole body, individual legs or back legs. The rabbit may also have lost bladder or bowel control.

Cause

Rabbits can injure their spine through improper handling. Individual legs can become paralysed during development. Elderly rabbits may develop problems associated with paralysis as their spinal column degenerates. Some rabbits become paralysed around their back legs once they are infected with *Toxoplasma gondii* and *Encephalitozoon cuniculi*, but this is quite rare.

Treatment

If a rabbit is badly paralysed or has injured its spine quite badly, euthanasia may be the kindest option. Rabbits are able to survive with one paralysed leg but more than one, particularly if one is a front leg, can have a detrimental effect on the rabbit's welfare. Looking after a rabbit with a spinal injury is very time consuming, as the rabbit may need to be held as it eats and drinks as well as injected to ensure that they are receiving the appropriate vitamins.

Prevention

To prevent a rabbit injuring its spine during handling, owners must spend time accustoming the rabbit to being handled and ensure that they are always lifting them in a manner that makes them feel safe. Feeding a diet high in vitamins and minerals, such as calcium and vitamins A and D may prevent the onset of age-related problems.

Leg damage around rabbit rings

Symptoms

Rabbit ring has become tight and the leg has become inflamed and raw.

Cause

Breeders in the UK mark their rabbits with a metal ring that is placed around one of the back legs when the rabbit is young so that it cannot drop off when they are older. Rings on rabbits that are not shown must be checked regularly to ensure that they have not become tight.

Treatment

Firstly the ring will be removed using special cutters. If the rabbit is to carry on being shown the owner should report the incident to the British Rabbit Council who will discuss other ways of marking the rabbit. The rabbit may have to be sedated to remove the ring in severe cases and owners must be careful to keep the rabbit's wound away from flies to prevent fly strike on the leg.

Prevention

Rabbits that are not being shown do not need to wear rings so they should be removed. Rabbit rings should be checked regularly to ensure that they have not become tight or caught.

Poisonous plants

Symptoms

Rabbits will be lethargic and may be stretched out. In extreme cases, they may have a fit or suffer organ failure.

Cause

Many household or garden plants can be toxic to rabbits, and as rabbits are not able to vomit they suffer the symptoms of poisoning.

Treatment

In cases where the rabbit has eaten less toxic plants, the rabbit should recover if they are kept warm and given access to hay and fresh water. In more extreme cases the rabbit may need to be treated within a veterinary practice.

Prevention

Rabbits should not be allowed to consume plants that grow from bulbs (for example crocuses, bluebells, daffodils), anemones, bracken, buttercups, celandine, convolvulus (Bindweed), Deadly Nightshade, docks, figwort, foxglove, hellebore, hemlock, all irises, Lily of the Valley, oak leaves, poppies, privet, ragwort, Toadflax, laburnum, lupins, primroses, rhododendron and wild celery. This list is not exhaustive so rabbits should not be allowed unsupervised access in a garden or area that contains unknown plants.

Heat stroke

Symptoms

The rabbit might be struggling to breathe or appear to be breathing through their mouth. They will be very weak as well as uncoordinated. In severe cases the rabbit might have convulsions and die.

Cause

Housing the rabbit in direct sunlight with no shade and poor ventilation. Long journeys in a hot car or being left in a stationary car on a warm day can also cause heat stroke.

Treatment

The rabbit's body should be sprayed with lukewarm water as soon as it is found. The rabbit should then be taken to a vet who may give the rabbit fluid to counteract the dehydration and medication to aid recovery.

Prevention

Rabbits should always have lots of ventilation and shade. Even winter sun can warm up a room or car. If rabbits have to travel in a car they should be given fresh air and water regularly and not be left in a stationary car for any length of time.

Administering medication

Treating a rabbit with prescribed medication is easier if a friend or family member holds them. If the rabbit is likely to struggle, it can be wrapped in a towel to keep it still and protect the handler from any scratches.

Tablets

Open the mouth and place the tablet towards the back of the tongue. Gently massage the throat to encourage the rabbit to swallow. Alternatively break the tablet into small pieces and hide each one within a small piece of banana, which can then be fed to the rabbit by hand.

Ear drops

Hold the ears vertically and gently insert, not push, the tip of the bottle into the ear canal. Slightly squeeze the bottle to release the drops, remove the bottle and massage the ears to spread the medication throughout the ear.

Eye ointment

Gently open the eye and apply a line of the ointment along the bottom edge of the lid, as if you were applying eyeliner.

Eye drops

Gently open the eye and insert the required number of drops into the corner of the lower lid.

Creams

Clean the wound using warm, salty water and cotton wool. Apply the cream to the wound, starting in the centre and moving outwards.

Syrup

Gently open the rabbit's mouth and place the dropper into the corner of the rabbit's mouth, angled towards the throat. Slowly release the required number of drops.

Post-operative care

Your veterinary practice will provide you with a list of recommendations if your rabbit has had an operation. These include:

- keeping the rabbit in a warm environment for the first 24 to 48 hours
- checking the wound daily during the winter and twice a day during the summer months to protect against fly strike
- if the rabbit lives outdoors, changing the bedding to newspaper or woodchip until the wound has healed. Sawdust and straw can cause irritations
- offering them their normal food and some water as soon as they return home.

Neutering

Many rabbits are neutered for the practical reasons of preventing unwanted pregnancies, removing some unwanted behaviours and improving temperament, but there are also health benefits, particularly for females.

Spaying female rabbits involves removing the uterus and ovaries and this can prevent uterine infections and adenocarcinoma. The operation is quite standard nowadays but the doe may still take a couple of days to recover from the operation and care must be taken to ensure that she does not try to remove her stitches.

Castrating a male rabbit removes the testicles and is a relatively quick operation. The male rabbit can recover quickly and, as the stitches are likely to be dissolvable, the rabbit may not need to go back to the veterinary surgery.

If rabbits are to be paired after castration or spaying, this should not take place until at least four weeks after the operation to prevent stored sperm from impregnating an entire doe or injuries caused by mounting.

Elderly rabbits

Rabbits can live for between five and ten years, depending on the breed. As a rabbit approaches its twilight years, several physical changes can occur, including a reduction in energy levels and a loss of coat quality. At this time, health checks made by the owner or the vet need to be more regular and very thorough. In general, older animals require more stability and security and are not as adaptable as younger animals so a rabbit may not accept changes to its home environment or routine as well as it used to. This is an important consideration when pairing rabbits or introducing a child or other pet.

Introducing a younger rabbit to the older rabbit to 'give him a new lease of life' may backfire slightly as older animals are often more intolerant of youthful exuberance. It may be wiser to get an adult rabbit as a companion if this seems appropriate.

Saying goodbye

Deciding to put an animal to sleep is never an easy decision. Sometimes the choice is made simpler because the rabbit is very sick, unable to perform basic functions, or is unlikely to get better.

The vet is often the best person to consult at this time – helping owners to make the right decision based on the rabbit's quality of life and the likelihood of any treatment offering a long-term solution. Organizations, such as the Rabbit Welfare Association offer bereavement support (see 'Taking it further').

Grieving is a natural process and not an emotion to shy away from. Pets become companions and as such become a part of the family. They are always sorely missed.

welfare

In this chapter you will learn:

- **how welfare affects domestic rabbits**
- **about areas of concern**
- **what stress is.**

'The Welfare of an individual is its state as regards its attempts to cope with its environment'

Professor Donald Broom, professor of Animal Welfare in the Department of Clinical Veterinary Medicine, University of Cambridge

The concept of welfare varies from person to person – from the perception that the animal's needs are being met adequately through its environment, regular feeding and a water supply, through to whether the animal is able to perform natural behaviours. Of course, a compromise is often reached between the needs of the animal and the abilities of the owner but a realistic assessment of what space, resources and time you can give to keeping rabbits is fundamental to preventing welfare problems.

Indicators of welfare

Assessing welfare adequately should not be driven purely by human emotions but should be based on a thorough understanding of the behaviour and physiology of the animal in question. Behaviour is often a reliable indicator of welfare as it is modified by the animal to enable them to cope with the situations that they find themselves in.

The Five Freedoms

In 1966, the UK government's Brambell Report suggested that farm animals should be given certain freedoms; these five freedoms have been promoted by the Farm Animal Welfare Council (FAWC) and are incorporated into the welfare codes used by the UK Department of Environment, Fisheries and Rural Agriculture (Defra) as well as the providing the criteria for the RSPCA's Freedom Food logo. Most importantly, they offer an easy guide for owners of any animals as they can be placed alongside knowledge of the natural behaviour and physiology.

The Five Freedoms are:

Freedom from hunger and thirst: provide ready access to fresh water and a diet that maintains full health and vigour.

Freedom from discomfort: provide an appropriate environment including shelter and a comfortable resting area.

Freedom from pain, injury or disease: prevention or rapid diagnosis and treatment.

Freedom to express normal behaviour: provide sufficient space, proper facilities and the company of the animal's own kind.

Freedom from fear: ensure conditions and treatment which avoid mental suffering.

Areas of consideration for domestic rabbits

The following recommendations are based on the information provided throughout this book and are by no means complete.

Pets

- Rabbits should not be purchased on impulse.
- It is not sensible to buy a rabbit as a present for a child who may lose interest.
- Buy a rabbit from a reputable source and try not to buy any that do not look well. To do so will encourage that person to sell more rabbits in the future.
- One of the worst things to happen to a rabbit is for it to be kept alone in a hutch at the end of the garden because everyone has lost interest.
- Owners should avoid re-homing a rabbit due to a lack of understanding of natural behaviour or requirements.
- Rabbits that are released into the countryside once they are no longer required will not mix in with the wild population and live happily ever after. They will die very quickly as they are unable to survive for long when they have to find their own shelter and food.

Nutrition

- Rabbits should be fed a diet that is high in fibre and is completely herbivorous.
- They should be allowed to graze on appropriate vegetable matter, ideally hay or grass.
- Food and water should be replenished regularly.
- Pregnant and lactating does as well as young rabbits need to be fed slightly differently to other rabbits, as their nutritional requirements are different.

- Overweight rabbits are unable to clean themselves, feed properly and are at risk from numerous health problems, many fatal.
- Selective feeding (eating just the best bits of the rabbit mix) means that the rabbit is not getting adequate fibre, vitamins and minerals.
- Treats that are high in harmful sugars or saturated fats, such as chocolate biscuits, increase the risk of rabbits becoming overweight but are also likely to upset their delicate digestive system.

Housing

- Rabbits should be housed in an environment that keeps them safe from predators.
- Their home should give them enough space to be able to move around freely. Ideally they should be able to stand on their back legs and take two or three hops in any given direction.
- All rabbit housing should protect the occupants from the elements whilst providing adequate ventilation.
- Rabbits should be cleaned out regularly and always have access to dry bedding.
- Space allocations should be increased if the number of individuals rises – a doe and litter should be given more space than a single rabbit.
- Wooden hutches must be treated with an animal-friendly preservative or stain.
- Housing should be located in a cool and quiet area of the home or garden.
- Rabbits should be given regular exercise, in an enclosed run or on the floor of a shed.

General care

- Medium- and long-haired rabbits must be groomed regularly.
- Nails should be kept neatly trimmed.
- Rabbits should be taken to the vet for regular vaccinations and health checks.
- The rabbit's environment should not attract flies and other pests.
- The owner should check the rabbit regularly to assess overall health.

- In the home, rabbits should be kept away from electric wires and other furnishings that could harm them if chewed.
- Rabbits should be prevented from eating poisonous house or garden plants.
- Indoor rabbits should be kept away from radiators and draughts.

Social contact

- Rabbits require regular social contact, preferably with a member of their own species.
- If rabbits are handled in a way that makes them feel safe then they are less likely to feel fearful or injure themselves by struggling.
- Although rabbits should live with another rabbit, they should be separated if they are being bullied or injured during fights. Once the problems have been identified and addressed the rabbits can be reintroduced.
- Rabbits must be supervised every time they are with the pet dog or cat as well as with small children.
- Rabbits that are handled regularly when they are young and throughout early adulthood are less likely to develop into rabbits that are scared of people.
- To prevent fear and distress, rabbits should not be punished by their owner.

Breeding

- When rabbits are due to give birth they should be left alone. Other people and animals should also be kept away from the hutch.
- Rabbits should be fed appropriately during pregnancy and when lactating.
- A lactating doe must be given continual access to water as she will drink more at this time.
- The use of nest boxes or removing the doe from the hutch for short periods of time will enable her to exhibit normal parenting behaviour.
- Repeated inbreeding of individuals to their parents or siblings can lead to health problems and reduced fertility.
- Breeders should try to improve their strain by not breeding from rabbits with poor temperaments or health problems.

Exhibiting

- Train your rabbit to be comfortable with handling and travelling in a car before you go to a show.
- If it is a hot day try to do the majority of the driving when it is cooler and stop regularly. Place the travel boxes in an open area to allow the passage of air around and through them.
- Check your rabbit's leg ring every week to ensure that it is not causing discomfort.
- It is a British Rabbit Council rule that rabbits have access to water at shows. It is also advisable to give them some hay in the pen so that they have something to keep them occupied as well as keeping their digestive system moving.
- Trancing (see below) is not recommended as a way of examining the underside of the rabbit and should not be performed for entertainment purposes.
- If you are exhibiting a large breed rabbit, ask the show secretary for a large pen when you enter.
- Check that your rabbit's pen is safe and secure. Ensure that the lid closes and that the rabbit cannot lift it. Also check the sides are secured adequately and could not be pushed over by a neighbouring rabbit.

Health

- Remove any animal with an illness or apparent problem to a 'quarantine' area and treat the problem immediately.
- Perform regular health checks on a daily, weekly and monthly basis.
- Feed your rabbit on as natural a diet as possible to prevent digestive, tooth and eye problems.
- Reduce any stressors (see below) to help prevent disease.
- Keep your rabbit's hutch clean and check its bottom regularly to reduce the risks of fly strike.
- Be prepared to have your rabbit put to sleep if its quality of life becomes adversely affected by an illness.

Trancing rabbits

Rabbits can be put into a trance-like state when they are laid on their backs. This is widely used in veterinary practice for minor procedures and by breeders and owners alike to aid in the removal or leg rings, to check nails and teeth or even as a party-piece. When the rabbit is in a 'trance' it is a state known as tonic immobility that is fear-driven and evolved to be used against predators to limit injury and enable escape – the predator may lose interest if the prey appears to be dead.

Studies have shown that physical indicators of stress, such as elevations in respiration, heart rate and plasma corticosterone, were recorded following tonic immobility. The body, to reduce the effects of stress, releases plasma corticosterone. Behaviours associated with fear, such as wide eyes, flattened ears, over-struggling and increased tension in the muscles, were also recorded as the rabbit was put into a trance. Following the trance, the rabbits showed increased levels of grooming and hiding behaviours. The conclusion of the study (by McBride *et al.*, 2006) was that the recorded physiological and behavioural responses of rabbits to tonic immobility indicated a stress state.

Although tonic immobility is part of the rabbit's repertoire of natural behaviour, there is concern over the use of tonic immobility at times when good handling or husbandry would suffice. Its use as a 'trick' is of particular welfare concern.

Stress

The term stress is often used to cover a range of feelings but the correct use is to describe a situation in which environmental conditions are having an adverse effect on an individual. Stress is a state, the environmental factors that lead to stress are stressors and the individuals under stress show stress responses.

figure 15 a rabbit's stress can be read in its body posture

There are many factors that influence the response of an individual to stress; these include previous experience and/or familiarity of the stressor, genetic predisposition and individual susceptibility.

Stressful situations are usually associated with a lack of control and can be particularly severe if the individual is unable to predict events. The most stressful situations for animals are often those that would be most diligently avoided in the wild – this consideration is of paramount importance to the rabbit, a prey animal.

Examples of stressors that may affect rabbits:

- Novelty – examples include the first trip in a car, the first visit to a show, handling by a 'stranger'.
- Fear-inducing stimuli – examples include sudden noises, other animals or poor handling.
- Social stress – examples include a lack of social contact or interactions with many individuals in a limited space.
- Inability to perform normal behaviour patterns – examples includes a lack of social contact, exercise, or an inability to retreat from a stressor.
- Pain, discomfort or illness.
- Anticipation of pain or discomfort – examples include poor or excessive handling.
- Inability to control environmental factors – examples includes poor ventilation, temperatures at shows, travelling in a car on a hot day, and poorly lit shed.
- Lack of space – examples include hutches, indoor cages and show pens.
- Withdrawal of food or water.

Behaviour patterns occurring in response to various stressors include:

- Fear related behaviour – as a prey species, rabbits are likely to freeze when a fear-inducing stimulus is encountered. This may be associated with a decrease in heart rate and an increase in rapid breathing. If they have space, rabbits will also try to hide or flee from the stressor. If there appears little option they may use aggression. Occasionally displacement activities are used to deal with stress – for example chewing novel items.
- Anxiety related behaviour – anxiety lasts longer than fear and is usually associated with anticipation of an event or

interaction. Behavioural signs include jumpiness, frequent urination and defecation.

- Behaviour pattern due to frustration – barren environments are associated with abnormal behaviour patterns such as excessive destruction, over-grooming and self-directed aggression.
- Behaviour patterns due to position in social order – where rabbits are living in groups but have limited space and reduced access to food and water certain animals may become the target of aggression from other individuals.
- Separation behaviour – female rabbits and youngsters may display an increase in apathy and a decrease in social behaviours associated with sudden weaning.
- Apathy of depressed behaviour – rabbits in barren environments with no social contact can appear relatively unresponsive or lethargic.

rabbits and man

In this chapter you will learn:
- **how man first kept rabbits**
- **about the rabbits' involvement in songs and stories**
- **how to garden with rabbits.**

Man's relationship with the European rabbit, *Oryctolagus cuniculus* was first recorded by the Phoenicians over 1,000 years BCE, when they termed the Iberian Peninsula *i-shephan-im* ('the land of the rabbit'), which the Romans changed to the Latin form, *Hispania*, the origin of the modern word Spain.

However, rabbits and people interact in many different ways and we have a unique relationship with these animals – we hate them if they eat our crops or damage our gardens, we eat them, accidentally hit them in our cars, wear them, use them to make sure our cosmetics and medicines are safe and yet they are a very common pet, much loved by their owners as well as being characterized as popular cartoon characters and contributing to some of our oldest traditions.

Rabbits as a source of food

Although the Normans introduced the rabbit into Britain as a source of meat and fur, the Romans kept wild rabbits in *leporaria*, originally used for keeping hares and other wild animals. Rabbits were hunted for food as a sport in these early game parks. The Romans transported the rabbit throughout the Roman Empire as a game animal, but it has been suggested that the rabbits dug their way out of the enclosures and colonized these countries more by accident than design.

Rabbit is thought to feature in the recipes of Apicius, the Roman chef and gourmet author of the only surviving Roman cookery book, *De Re Coquinaria* (meaning 'The Art of Cooking'). The Romans associated the rabbit with Venus and believed eating its meat granted beauty. They also believed a diet of rabbit meat could cure impotence or infertility, totally understandable given the rabbit's well-known rate of reproduction. Because a rabbit or hare was usually the first animal to give birth in the spring, it was associated with rebirth and vitality with many tombs and paintings showing rabbit-like animals eating figs and grapes, also symbols of rebirth.

The first mention of rabbits on the British Isles is in a report on the Scilly Isles in 1176 so it has been suggested that the Norman crusaders brought the rabbit back to Britain at the end of the twelfth century. In the early part of the twelfth century unborn and newborn rabbits were exempt from a papal decree that prevented Catholics eating meat during Lent. It is thought that the Catholic monks who kept wild rabbits in the monastery courtyard and removed the young as a regular, cheap, food source first domesticated rabbits.

Historical records have charted the status of the rabbit as a food source to man over the years. The parkland of Hampton Court Palace was used to farm rabbits to help raise money for the crusades in the twelfth century and Henry III is thought to have served no less than 450 rabbits (along with many other animals) at one feast whilst Elizabeth I had several rabbit 'islands' that she used for hunting wild rabbits.

From the fifteenth century on it was common practice for explorers to take breeding rabbits on explorations as a food source and release them onto islands to provide a supply of fresh meat. The rabbit is now found throughout Europe, South America and Australasia.

Domestication took place with rabbits being bred for their size (meat yield) and the quality of their fur. As rabbits could be kept easily and cheaply, grew quickly, bred in captivity and produced a fair amount of meat, the art of backyard rabbit keeping was born with people keeping a couple of domestic rabbits for the table. In time, rabbits were bred for exhibition, being judged on the quality of the carcass and the pelt (skin with fur attached).

Rabbit meat was not rationed during the Second World War and previous attempts to control the numbers of wild rabbits were relaxed during the war – perhaps due to a reduced work force but certainly to increase its availability. Rabbit meat is relatively low in fat and high in protein and is also a good source of niacin, iron, phosphorus, and vitamin B12. In Victorian times, whilst roast beef and goose was the Christmas dinner of choice, turkeys being too expensive for the majority to enjoy, many underprivileged people ate rabbit.

Commercial rabbit farming in the UK has suffered from the increasing status of the rabbit as a pet animal, people's reluctance to eat this once much loved meat and its associations with wartime rationing. In the rest of the world, rabbits are farmed in large numbers for their meat, particularly in China, Hungary and Poland.

Rabbit fur

Wearing rabbit has gone in and out of fashion despite the rabbit's continual relationship with man since Norman times.

During the process of domestication some breeds were created for their fur, these include Rex rabbits, the Beveren and the Angora. The Angora rabbit provides wool whereas the other rabbits were bred for their pelts that were considered luxurious. At one time pelts of the Rex commanded high prices in the fur industry.

The rabbit fur and wool industry was very popular in the 1920s with its use in scarves, glove linings and full-length coats as well as providing felt for hats. Bowler hats, first designed in 1850, used rabbit fur as the sole felting material until they slumped in popularity during the 1960s.

In Australia 'rabbiters' trapped rabbits commercially for their skins during the 1930s and 40s. At one stage rabbit pelts were worth more than a sheepskin. The pelts were processed into fur felt, and made into hats worn by the Australian Diggers in the Second World War. Today, the traditional Australian Akubra hats are made from rabbit fur felt.

With the rise of the anti-fur lobby in the 1980s came the demise of fur wearing in the UK, although it continues throughout Europe. In recent years, rabbit fur has been back in fashion within the UK with the trend for Mukluk boots in 2005 and the introduction of rabbit fur onto the high street as coat collars and gilet waistcoats.

The wool industry has faired better in the popularity stakes although there are concerns over the welfare of rabbits in wool farms in Asia. Shearing or plucking Angora rabbits produces Angora wool that is spun to produce yarn. Angora wool is often confused with the Angora goat, which produces mohair.

Rabbits as pests

Rabbits have successfully colonized the countries that they have been introduced into. It is testament to the rabbit as a species that they have been able to survive and increase in numbers in a variety of habitats. Often, this is as a direct result of the low number of native predators to that country.

However, rabbits are viewed as pests by many landowners due to the destruction wreaked by burrows and grazing. The problem of rabbit infestations was documented by Roman historian and geographer Strabo, who gave the following account of non-native rabbits introduced in the second century BCE into the Gymnesiae (now known as the Baleriac islands of Menorca, Mallorca and Ibiza).

> 'No injurious animal can easily be found in the Gymnesiae. For even the rabbits there, it is said, are not native, but the stock sprang from a male and female brought over by some person from the opposite mainland [of coastal Spain]; and this stock was, for a fact, so numerous at first, that they even overturned houses and trees by burrowing beneath them ...'
>
> (III.5.2)

One country plagued by rabbits relatively recently is Australia, where rabbits were introduced as a food supply by the first fleet in 1788 although many sources feel that the rabbits in today's Australia can be traced back to just 24 rabbits that were released onto a property in Victoria for hunting purposes. The Australian politician, Sir Henry Parkes (1815–96) is said to have offered a £25,000 reward for a solution to the country's rabbit infestation.

The solution didn't arrive until 1953 in the form of Myxomatosis. This was first introduced into France where it killed high numbers of domestic and wild rabbits. It was intentionally introduced into the UK and Australia to control wild rabbit populations. Initial estimates were that the wild rabbit population in Australia dropped from 600 million to 100 million whilst almost 90 per cent of the UK's wild rabbits were dead by 1955 along with approximately 40 per cent of the domestic rabbits being produced for consumption.

Myxomatosis is a highly lethal disease caused by the Myxoma virus and spread by biting insects. It was first described in 1898 in Uruquay where it was seen to kill large numbers of the European rabbit. The disease causes the rabbit to develop swellings and nodules on the eyes, ears, nose and genitals that cause blindness and deafness; eventually the emaciated rabbit dies of a secondary infection such as pneumonia.

Although wild rabbits are still seen infected with Myxomatosis, some strains have developed a genetic immunity to the virus. A vaccine for domestic rabbits was developed and has been used quite successfully in the UK for many years, although the vaccinating of domestic rabbits is illegal in Australia due to concerns that the live virus will be passed into wild population's thereby increasing immunity.

In the early 1990s, VHD virus (Rabbit Calcivirus) was controversially introduced into Australia and New Zealand to help control wild populations of rabbits that were starting to increase in areas that were low in natural mosquito populations (mosquitoes are the main carriers of Myxomatosis from rabbit to rabbit).

VHD causes the sudden death of rabbits, often in pain but with few external signs. Essentially the virus causes the death of cells within the liver and haemorrhages within the lungs and kidney. Sometimes rabbits that have died of VHD have blood around the nose, mouth and anus.

As the VHD virus is passed by contact so it has greater potential in controlling rabbit numbers. Domestic rabbits can be vaccinated against the disease, even in Australia, as the vaccine uses a dead virus that cannot replicate within the rabbit's body.

In the UK, VHD became the first notifiable rabbit disease after it first appeared in the UK in the early 1990s. The notification and restrictions were lifted by MAFF (Ministry of Agriculture, Fisheries and Food – now known as Defra) in 1996 once a vaccine had been licensed for use during 1994.

Other methods for managing wild rabbit populations include the use of ferrets (to flush rabbits out of their burrows where they are then caught in nets or by dogs), the use of traps and shooting.

Rabbits and research

The rabbit has become a popular laboratory animal due to its size and nature, because it can be obtained easily, housed and fed simply and is able to breed in captivity. The rabbit's high rate of reproduction has enabled laboratories to breed their own populations of domestic breeds that may show characteristics useful to the study.

The rabbits specialized reproductive system also means that the time of ovulation can be determined exactly (as it occurs ten hours after mating) making rabbits the subject for many early studies on genetics as well as the animal of choice for studies on reproduction and development in mammals.

Rabbits are commonly used as a test animal for the safety of medicinal products and in eye irritation experiments (known as the Draize Eye Test) but have also been used to investigate cystic fibrosis, tuberculosis, arteriosclerosis and asthma. It is estimated that in 2004 over 20,000 rabbits were used for animal testing in the UK.

Using animals for research is a very emotive area, but increasing public pressure and an awareness of the limitations surrounding the testing of products for human use on animals has led to the introduction of strict controls on the requirements for licensing and support into the use of alternatives, such as tissue cultures. The UK Home Office state: 'We have legislated so experimentation is only permitted when there is no alternative research technique and the expected benefits outweigh any possible adverse effects'.

During their time in laboratories, rabbits have been the subject of many studies into group housing, space allocation and the impact of early experience, all of which have contributed to the welfare of subsequent populations as well as increasing understanding of our pet rabbits' needs.

Rabbits and the garden

It is fair to say that rabbits and gardeners are not the best of friends. In fact, rabbits are not popular with any landowners due to their tendency to selectively feed, dig holes and damage large areas of land.

Discouraging rabbits from your garden or land is extremely difficult – rabbit-proof fencing has to be buried at least 30cm (12¼ in) below the ground and the mesh has to be no more than 3cm (1¼ in) wide to stop young rabbits getting through. To stop rabbits going over the fence, it should be a metre high.

Rabbit-proof fencing is quite a skill and some people prefer to admit defeat and plant in a way that discourages rabbits – plants such as Snapdragons (*Antirrhinum majus*), the Michaelmas Daisy (*Aster novi-bel*gii), Lily of the Valley (*Convollaria majalis*) and Sweet Williams (*Dianthus barbatus*) are considered to be disliked by rabbits.

Some gardeners place spiky plant clippings or Epsom salts around the base of plants to deter the rabbits whilst others cover their saplings in plastic protectors or invest in outdoor ultrasound pest repellers, but rabbits will usually find a way to reach the plants that they want to eat.

The only element of the rabbit that interests the gardener is their faeces as they are very high in nitrogen and a good source of potash making it an excellent fertilizer for flowers or vegetables and a useful contribution to the composting process (for more information on composting see Chapter 06).

Rabbits and our culture

Although rabbits have only recently been domesticated as pets, they have a long history with man that has led to an involvement in our entertainment, traditions, superstitions and art.

There are many rabbit cartoon characters that have become much-loved cultural figures and storytellers. Br'er Rabbit was the hero of African–American folktales of the southern states of America (Br'er derives from the habit of addressing another man as 'brother' in many African cultures). Enid Blyton wrote a Brer Rabbit series (1938) based on a cute and crafty rabbit that outwitted his enemies with his tricks. Bugs Bunny's character was a bullied but street-wise rabbit that wreaks havoc on characters such as Elmer Fudd and Wile E. Coyote. Rabbit in *Winnie the Pooh* (written in the 1920s) is a very wise animal who protects his precious garden from other animals whilst Roger Rabbit, from the 1988 Disney film *Who framed Roger Rabbit?* was portrayed as a friendly, innocent character (with a very voluptuous wife, Jessica) framed for a murder.

Probably closer to the natural life of the rabbit are the stories of Peter Rabbit, who first appeared in 1901 when Beatrix Potter introduced him as he set about eating all the vegetables in Mr McGregor's garden. Similarly Richard Adams's *Watership Down* (1972) followed the story of a group of rabbits fleeing the destruction of their home to property developers.

With its obvious ability to breed successfully, the rabbit has been used in art and tradition to represent love and lust. There are many famous paintings showing the rabbit with Venus, the goddess of love, and the Madonna. These include Francesco del Cossa's 1470s mural the *Garden of Love* on the walls of the Palazzo Schifanio in Ferrara (Italy), Piero di Cosimo's *Venus, Mars and Cupid* (1490) and Titian's *Madonna and the Rabbit* (1530).

Of course, the modern-day representation of the rabbit as the symbol of lust is as the *Playboy* logo. It is said that Hugh Hefner, the founder of Playboy magazine, suggested the rabbit as he felt it was cute, sexy and frisky.

The Easter Bunny started out as a hare in pre-Christian times when festivals were held around the 21 March (the start of spring) to celebrate Eastre, the goddess of dawn and fertility. The festival continued, through Christian times, with the name changed to Easter and rabbits and eggs symbolizing fertility and new beginnings.

Carrying a rabbit's foot in your pocket for luck goes back many centuries but its exact origin is not clear, although it is thought to be a southern United States tradition. There are many theories which include that the foot was thought to be considered lucky because the rabbit's hind feet went before its front legs when it ran, that to own any part of an animal associated with productiveness assured good luck and that when trapping animals a rabbit was often caught before larger animals (such as foxes that presumably would be using the same routes) so catching a rabbit was a sign of forthcoming luck and the foot was kept as this was the part caught in the trap.

In the Middle Ages, the monthly cycle of the moon assumed great importance, so any farmers or hunters who wanted to ensure good luck in the coming cycle would repeat talismanic oaths. On the first of the month, prayers were said to the primitive gods for good luck, such as 'Rabbit, rabbit, rabbit'; or 'lucky rabbit, lucky rabbit', or, because of the association of the colour white with the sun and with virtue, 'white rabbit, white rabbit, white rabbit'.

The well-known song

'Run, rabbit, run, rabbit, run, run, run.
Run, rabbit, run, rabbit, run, run, run.
Bang, bang, bang, bang, goes the farmer's gun.
Run, rabbit, run, rabbit, run, run, run.

Run, rabbit, run, rabbit, run, run, run.
Don't give the farmer his fun, fun, fun.
He'll get by without his rabbit pie,
So run, rabbit, run, rabbit, run, run, run.'

Was adapted during the Second World War to raise morale by including the words:

'Run Adolf, Run Adolf, Run, Run, Run,
Don't give the farmer his fun, fun, fun!
He'll get by without his rabbit pie
Run Adolf, Run Adolf, Run, Run, Run.'

In the Chinese calendar, the rabbit is one of twelve animals used to symbolize a calendar year. Legend has it that as Buddha was about to depart the earth he summoned all the animals to say goodbye. Only twelve turned up so, to show his appreciation of their loyalty, he vowed that from then on each year would bear the name of one of the animals. People born during the year of the rabbit (1939, 1951, 1963, 1975, 1987, 1999 and 2001) are said to be clean and neat, quiet and often softly spoken. They dislike conflict and will go to great lengths to avoid discord. 'Rabbits' thrive in tranquil, harmonious settings and become unhappy in noisy, argumentative company.

Rabbits as pets

When we look at the physical appearance of breeds like the Angora, the Dutch or the English Lop, it is hard to believe that they all originate from the European wild rabbit. Domestication and the process of selective breeding rabbits, for size, ear position and coat colour started around 1500 years ago. With dogs, domestication starting around 12,000 years ago – our rabbits are relative newcomers to the pet scene!

The animals that have been successfully domesticated by man usually have certain characteristics that aid the process. These include a willingness to approach humans, a social hierarchy, the ability to breed successfully in captivity and a pleasant disposition. The initial domestication of rabbits as a meat source reduced the importance of confidence and a good temperament but these traits were selected once rabbits were bred for use as laboratory or exhibition animals.

With the increasing interest in rabbit fur and the subsequent rise of the rabbit fancy came the breeding together of individuals that exhibited certain physical characteristics such as coat quality and colour, markings, ear length and position and the size of rabbit.

The Victorians first started to keep rabbits as pets. As a pet, the rabbit was saved from the table and becoming someone's coat. Pet rabbits were not shown and lived in hutches in the garden, usually tended by the children. In these early days of pet rabbits, their status was pretty low and they were readily replaced if anything untoward happened to them. This attitude continues in some families to this day, but during the 1980s the importance of the rabbit as a companion animal started to increase.

Many people have kept rabbits indoors but the rise of the 'house rabbit' during the late 1980s and early 1990s changed the status of rabbits from cuddly meat animal to a complex pet. As a consequence, the new breed of rabbit owner lavished care and attention on their pet and expected specialized veterinary knowledge.

Vets with a special interest in rabbits were once hard to find, but now most practices have one or more members of staff able to help. The increasing interest in the wellbeing and health of the rabbit also led to the diversification of pet behaviour counsellors to help owners understand and improve their pet's behaviour.

The American House Rabbit Society was born in 1988 and in 1996 the British House Rabbit Association (now the Rabbit Welfare Association) was formed to improve the quality of life of pet rabbits in the UK. They aim to achieve this by:

> '... advancing the education of the public in the care and ownership of domestic rabbits kept as pets in Britain and to further advance the knowledge of rabbit medicine amongst the UK veterinary profession. Conducting or promoting the conduct of clinical research and then publishing the useful results of such research into specific health projects in order to increase understanding of common health problems in domestic rabbits. The RWF only funds humane research. We prefer to support clinical studies which benefit the rabbit taking part, as well as providing answers that will help our rabbits'.

With expert veterinary care available, information sheets and books on sale in most pet shops and bookstores, a wealth of useful information in magazines and on the internet, as well as through rabbit organizations, it is amazing that so many people are not aware of the realities of having a rabbit and feel unable to keep them.

Mairwen Guard of Cottontails Rabbit and Guinea Pig Rescue (see 'Taking it further') surveyed 200 UK rescue centres in 1997 and estimated that 24,000 rabbits were put up for adoption in that year. A later survey by the Rabbit Welfare Association gave a figure of 33,000 rabbits that had been taken into rescue shelters although they acknowledge that this figure only represents the tip of the iceberg as there are no details on the number of rabbits rehomed privately, set free in the fields to fend for themselves or put to sleep by veterinary practices.

The Royal Society for the Prevention of Cruelty to Animals (RSPCA) were involved in just under 5,000 UK rabbit cases during 2005 – whether abandonment, road traffic accidents, trappings, neglect or public complaints. Rabbits are the third most popular pets to be rehomed by the RSPCA and in 2004 over 10,000 rabbits were found new homes through national or branch establishments.

A study of 450 rabbit owners rehoming their rabbits through Cottontails Rabbit and Guinea Pig Rescue found that over a quarter of all rabbits handed into rescue centres had already had at least two previous homes. Almost 60 per cent of these rabbits came from pet shops, just under 30 per cent from breeders, and about 10 per cent from animal rescue centres, garden centres, or handed in as strays. Most rabbits (32 per cent) were originally obtained for free, perhaps passed on by friends, relatives or neighbours. It appears from the data that whether the rabbit was free or cost the person £20 had little effect on the ultimate decision to give the pet away.

Although most of the rabbits in the study (60 per cent) were bought for children, 40 per cent were bought for adults. Mairwen also found that more female than male rabbits were placed for adoption (52 per cent versus 48 per cent). When asked who the rabbit was going to live with when it was first obtained, as many rabbits were bought to live on their own (46 per cent) as were bought to provide a companion for another rabbit (47 per cent).

Only (7 per cent) were bought to live with guinea pigs. Most of the rabbits being re-homed were aged between six months and one year (30 per cent), followed by one to two years (26 per cent), less than six months (22 per cent), and two to four years (19 per cent). Very few rabbits appear to be given up after four years (3 per cent). These figures would suggest that owners were most likely to re-home their rabbits around puberty and early adulthood when behaviour problems are most likely to develop.

Only 16 per cent of rabbits were neutered prior to their arrival at the rescue centre. Owners blamed the cost of vet fees, a lack of knowledge and apathy for the 84 per cent of rabbits arriving at rescue centres un-neutered. The most common reason given for re-homing was 'the children lost interest' and 'the novelty wore off' (36 per cent). Ignorance came next with 'didn't know how much time/work was involved' (20 per cent). The remaining categories were evenly distributed at about 10 per cent each: 'the rabbit was aggressive'; 'we are moving house';

'the rabbit is too expensive to keep'; 'we are going through a family break-up'; 'there is an illness/allergy'; 'we are going on holiday' or 'the rabbit has outgrown its hutch, not willing to buy another' contributed another 5 per cent.

A rabbit is likely to live for five to ten years and can become as close a companion as a dog or cat. If you are interested in keeping a rabbit, learn all you can before you make the decision and think about all the rabbits in rescue centres needing a home because someone didn't learn enough about them.

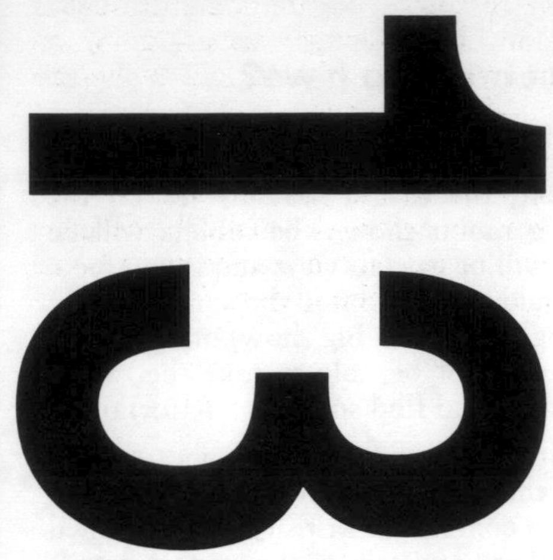

rabbit FAQs

In this chapter you will learn:

- **what to do with fussy eaters**
- **how to spot a phantom pregnancy**
- **when to replace your hutch.**

Finding a rabbit

How do I decide what breed to have?

There are many crossbreed rabbits that make perfect pets and are sometimes prone to less inherited problems, but if you are keen on a pure-bred rabbit, the easiest way to see all the different breeds is to visit a rabbit show. The rabbits will be shown within pens so they will be easy to view and if you see a breed that you like, you should be able to find the name of some breeders through the catalogue (if it is a big show) or by asking one of the stewards. You will not be able to take the rabbit home from the show but you could find some contact details.

Alternatively, some rabbit books have breed photos (see 'Recommended reading' in the 'Taking it further' section at the back of this book) or you can contact the British Rabbit Council or ARBA (see 'Taking it further') and ask for the contact details of a breeder in your area or the secretary of the National Club.

One breeder I have spoken to says that he does not handle the rabbits very often when they are young. Should I still have one of his?

Some rabbits are born with lovely temperaments regardless of handling, but to ensure that you do not end up with a rabbit that is scared of you I would suggest that you wait until you find a breeder that does handle his or her rabbits to ensure that they will make good pets.

If you are interested in showing a particular breed then you may be limited on your number of breeders. The British Rabbit Council and the ARBA will be able to put you in touch with the Secretary of the national breed club and they should help you with finding more breeders. Be prepared to travel to find the breeder and rabbit that is right for you.

The pet shop at the end of my road has lots of rabbits in a cage and I want to buy them to give them a good life. Is this wrong?

Although you are confident that you can give these rabbits a good life, the truth is that if you buy all of them you will show the pet shop that there is money to be had from selling rabbits and they will get more to sell. By all means talk to the shopkeeper about the rabbits and the advice that his customers are given – it might make you feel better if he or she seems genuinely caring.

Housing

My hutch is only one year old but the wood is rotting. What can I do?

Unless you are able to replace the piece of wood that is rotting you should put that hutch down to experience and purchase a more robust home that has been treated with an animal-friendly preservative and varnish to protect the wood from the weather and your rabbit's urine. Hutches are an expensive purchase but it is worth having one handmade or being prepared to pay a bit more so that you will have a home for your rabbit that lasts as long as they do.

My house rabbit doesn't go outside. Is that OK?

Rabbits need access to sunlight to keep them healthy and, as an outdoor animal, there is often a feeling that all rabbits should be given some time outside. Having said that, it is not only house rabbits that don't go outside; many breeding rabbits are kept in blocks of hutches or sheds. It is important that rabbits live in an area that is well ventilated and have access to natural light.

Rabbits that have lived inside for long periods may find the outdoors frightening so it is important to introduce them gradually using a run that has a covered end and placing it in a quiet and sheltered part of the garden.

My rabbit is a crossbreed. How do I get the right size hutch?

Assuming that your rabbit is now an adult and fully grown, measure him from nose to tail, preferably when he is resting and lying flat out so that you know how high your hutch should be. If you multiply it by two or three you will have the length.

Nutrition

My rabbit is a really fussy eater!

Some rabbits appear to be fussy with their food, feeding selectively on the pieces of food that they like most or not eating any hay. This can mean that they are not receiving enough fibre in their diet, as it is invariably the fibre that they leave behind. These rabbits may develop digestive problems (see Chapters 04 and Chapters 10) so it is really important to address this problem sooner rather than later.

If your rabbit eats lots of hay but selectively eats its mix, consider gradually changing over to an extruded pellet by mixing a smaller amount of the mix with a small amount of the pellets and don't replenish the bowl until it is empty. Eventually feed just pellets.

If your rabbit will only eat pellets or mix and refuses to eat hay, you may need to reduce the amount of concentrated food that he is being fed whilst increasing the amount of hay so that he has something to eat when he is hungry. With so many types of hay and cut grass now available it is also worth trying some different brands to see if you can find one that your rabbit likes the most. If your rabbit still won't eat a significant amount of hay then feeding a concentrated diet with high-fibre content (over 18 per cent) is acceptable along with some green plant matter.

If your rabbit will only eat hay and greens and does not like pellets or mixes, your rabbit's diet is very close to the wild rabbit and he should be very healthy so keep offering continual access to good quality hay.

I find the idea of pellets boring but my rabbit is a selective feeder. What are my options?

The first thing that you should do is shift the emphasis of your rabbit's diet onto a more natural basis by increasing the amount of hay and green leaves at the expense of the pellets or cereal mix. If your rabbit is then only picking out the 'best bits' this is less of a problem, as he should be getting enough fibre from the hay and vegetables. You should only replenish his bowl with a small amount of mix when it is empty and not be put off by the physical appearance of the pellets.

My rabbit loves bananas and mango. Is this bad?

Bananas and mango, as well as carrots, are full of natural sugars that can interfere with the rabbit's sensitive digestive system. Rabbits tend to love sugary foods but that does not mean that they are good for them, or us! A small amount of food that your rabbit really likes is not bad for training but, other than that, try to stick with green vegetables as treats.

I have read about environmental enrichment and would like to revamp my rabbit's hutch. Any tips on what I can do with food?

By its very definition, environmental enrichment covers ways that we can make the environment of our animals more stimulating and closer to the natural world. For rabbits this means introducing areas that they can hide in or behind alongside items that they can climb on or sit under. Changes can also be made to the way that we feed our rabbits so that they have to reach up to find food or spend longer periods of time grazing.

The easiest way to enrich a rabbit's environment is with the provision of hay, as this means that they have to spend time grazing. Cardboard boxes, tunnels, areas to dig and hanging green vegetables from the top of the run or door of the hutch are all simple but effective means of encouraging your rabbit to spend more time exploring his environment.

General care

My rabbit scratches when I pick her up. What can I do?

Initially, you should check your rabbit's nails so that they are not too sharp, but you could also consider wearing a long sleeved top or overcoat when you handle her. Rabbits often scratch us if they feel unstable during handling, so practise your handling so that you both feel more comfortable and confident.

I am scared of cutting my rabbit's nails myself. Who can I ask?

It is quite daunting the first time as we are all worried that we are going to cut too close to the quick and the rabbit will bleed. Once you have done your rabbit's nails successfully you will get used to the process and if you keep some styptic powder to hand that should stem any bleeding if you do make a mistake. Your vet or a vet nurse should be able to help you the first time and will check your rabbit's nails during the health check that is associated with vaccinations. Another person to help you is the person that you obtained your rabbit from.

How can I stop my rabbit digging out of her run?

Rabbits naturally dig as they live underground. Female rabbits are most likely to dig, particularly during the natural breeding season but we do not want our rabbits running free (or even living underground). You can cover the base of the run with sturdy wire although be aware that this can cause sore hocks and other injuries. If the behaviour does appear to be seasonal then neutering might help, although some rabbits are quite happy with a cardboard tube (from a roll of carpet) or a small sand pit to dig in.

My rabbit's hair is matted, what can I do?

Do not pull the mats as it is likely that you will do some damage to your rabbit's skin. Ideally the matted hair should be loosened gradually by starting at the top of the mat but if you are not intending to show your rabbit then gently clip the hair away.

Rabbits with matted fur are at a high risk of fly strike during the warmer months when flies are attracted to the faeces and urine that get caught up in the hair. It is essential that rabbits with medium to long hair be regularly groomed.

Health

I feed my rabbits on pellets but they seem to have diarrhoea. Should I change the brand of pellet?

Firstly, I would suggest that you take your rabbit to see your vet, as prolonged periods of diarrhoea should not be ignored. Your vet may advise a change of pellet but feeding your rabbit a more natural diet of hay and green leaves usually solves many dietary problems.

My rabbit struggles when I try to check her teeth. What can I do?

If your rabbit feels uncomfortable he/she will struggle to get away so the first thing to address is the way that you are holding him or her. Try to ensure that all four feet are on a flat surface or turn your rabbit onto his/her back and holding him/her in the crook of your arm. This is also a handy position for clipping nails, but your rabbit needs to be held safely. Some people wrap a towel around their rabbit so that they are protected and are not able to scratch the owner.

My vet trances my rabbit before he treats him. Is this safe?

Some vets feel that putting the rabbit into a trance, by laying them on their back, is less stressful than letting the rabbit experience the procedures. When a rabbit is in a trance it goes into a state called tonic immobility that is used to aid escape from a predator who might lose interest if the prey appears inactive. It is a very stressful state for the rabbit and should not be used at a time when better handling could suffice.

My rabbit seems to have been licked bald by my other rabbit. Why is this?

Rabbits have a tendency to groom each other and sometimes this can get out of hand leading to one individual losing more hair than the other. However, this level of grooming is often associated with teeth problems or a lack of fibre in the diet so a health check with the vet and an increase in the amount of hay that the rabbits are eating is advised.

Behaviour

My rabbit is aggressive towards me. Should I have him neutered?

If the aggression developed on or around the time of puberty and your rabbit was handled well as a youngster then neutering might help. Castrating a rabbit that is showing aggression through fear might have no effect on the behaviour, or could lead to an increase in the aggression. You should also work with your rabbit to change the apparent success of the aggression and to teach him some positive associations at times when he would normally be aggressive. For example, if your rabbit is always aggressive when you feed him then you should stop feeding him from one food bowl and offer lots of hay and a small amount of pellets or mix, perhaps put into two or three bowls. You should hand-feed your rabbit small amounts of vegetable as a treat and make sure that when you approach the hutch you are not looming over him and that you don't smell of any strong perfumes, or even of another rabbit.

Why does my rabbit thump its feet?

Rabbits in the wild thump their back legs on the ground quickly to signal danger. This sound causes all the members of the group to run for safety. When this behaviour is seen in a domestic situation, it would suggest that a rabbit is not happy and is concerned by an element of its environment. Offering places for the rabbit to hide, or moving it to another area might encourage relaxation.

My rabbit keeps urinating on the sofa. What should I do?

Rabbits often use urine to mark areas that smell strongly of themselves or of other individuals, so sofas are commonly anointed by house rabbits! On the other hand, a rabbit that has not been effectively toilet trained may start to use one area of the home as its latrine. Firstly, the sofa should be kept out of bounds for several weeks and cleaned thoroughly using a warm solution of a biological washing powder to reduce any residual smells. Your rabbit should be returned to his indoor cage for a period of several days to enable you to reinforce toilet training in his tray. Always use the same brand and style of litter so that your rabbit does not become confused. Gradually reintroduce your rabbit to the sofa, under supervision. If the problem persists, consider having your rabbit neutered, although sometimes age reduces the desire to mark quite so avidly.

Why does my rabbit zigzag round my feet?

Your rabbit is sizing you up as a potential mate! You might also hear your rabbit grunt and, if you're really 'lucky', you may get sprayed with urine.

Exhibiting

How do I find my nearest show?

Rabbit shows might be advertised locally in libraries or in local newspapers but all British Rabbit Council shows are listed in the magazine *Fur & Feather* (contact details are listed in the 'Taking it further' section of this book). The American Rabbits Breeders Association (ARBA) have a list of shows on their website (www.arba.net) or can put you in touch with the relevant secretary. The British Rabbit Council has a network of district advisers who would be able to help you find the nearest show to you and to help you find your way around.

How long do shows last?

For the average show, judging starts mid-morning and is finished by 4 pm. Of course the length of time for judging is dictated by the number of exhibits that have been entered but allow a full day as you are not able to take any rabbits home until after judging has finished.

Do I show under my name?

Under British Rabbit Council rules you can either show under your own name or you can have a stud name that should be one word, such as Pumpkin Stud.

Can my rabbit have food and water at a show and do I take my own bedding?

Your rabbit must have access to water throughout a show; to do otherwise is breaking a show rule. Judges should overlook a spot of water on a rabbit's coat.

Some feeds cause staining around the mouth or chin area so it is advised to feed your rabbit a pellet or mix after judging although hay should be made readily available all day to avoid any digestive disturbances caused by a lack of fibre.

A small amount of wood shavings will be provided at the show but you are advised to take some of your own bedding to fully cover the pen floor. Some fanciers use an absorbent material such as a square of VetBed or bring along straw. Avoid newspaper, as the ink can stain white feet or fur.

Breeding

My rabbit has rejected her young. What can I do?

Some does scatter their young around the hutch and will not move them back into the nest. If you find a kitten that is away from the nest, and still alive, then warm it in your hands (which should first be rolled in some dirty bedding so that they smell of the doe) and then return it to the nest and cover over the babies.

If you feel that your rabbit is not feeding the kittens, bearing in mind that it is normal for her to visit them only once every 20 hours, then you may need to consider fostering the young onto another doe that has a litter or hand-feeding them yourself. There is a step-by-step guide on hand-rearing in Chapter 08. If your doe seems unwell then take her to see your vet.

A healthy doe may reject her young if she feels that the environment is not stable or that she under threat from external stimuli. It is therefore very important that she is left alone in the week preceding the birth and that any activity is discouraged around the hutch during the first few weeks after the birth. If she rejects her young more than once, consider moving her to another hutch or not breeding from her again.

My rabbit is making a nest but hasn't been near a male. What is she doing?

It sounds as if she is having a phantom pregnancy. There is lots of information relating to this condition in Chapters 08 and 10, but in essence a female rabbit will display these behaviours when she hasn't been mated but has either been stroked quite vigorously around her back end, has been handled after an owner has been handling an entire male or if she has been mounted by a female rabbit that she might share a hutch or run with.

The nest is made much earlier in the cycle than in a true pregnancy – usually around day 16 or 17, rather than day 28 for example.

My rabbits won't breed – any tips?

Rabbits are thought to be able to breed many times all year long but this is not always the case and consideration for the time of year, the health of both individuals and the introduction process may be needed.

A fit and healthy buck and doe, which are not overweight or unhealthy, are very likely to mate easily and produce a vigorous litter of rabbits. Sometimes a buck and doe need to be left together for a period of time before they will mate so leaving them in the buck's hutch or in a run on the garden might just do the trick.

Rabbits that have been mated too much or too little may suffer from fertility problems as well as rabbits that are not fed appropriately (see Chapter 04). A doe might suffer a phantom pregnancy after an unsuccessful mating but is thought to be highly fertile once the effects have subsided and this is a good time to put her with the buck again.

Some breeders are able to mate their rabbits by intervention methods. These include artificial insemination and placing the buck's penis inside the doe but should not be performed unless absolutely necessary.

How many rabbits do I need to create my own stud?

There is no set number of rabbits; some people have as few as three breeding animals whereas other breeders can have over one hundred. To start a line, you can have one buck and two does (known as a 'trio') that you breed together, introducing in new individuals or line breeding over time (see Chapter 08). It is thought that twenty hutches is sufficient to successfully raise a line of one breed.

Useful organizations

ARBA (ARBA)
PO Box 426
Bloomington
IL 61702
USA
Tel. 001 (309) 664 7500
www.arba.net

Association of Pet Behaviour Counsellors (APBC)
PO Box 46
Worcester
WR8 9AB
Tel. 01386 751151
www.apbc.org.uk

British Rabbit Council (BRC)
Purefoy House
7 Kirkgate
Newark
Nottinghamshire
NG24 1AD
Tel. 01636 676042
www.thebrc.org

Composting Organization
Avon House
Tithe Barn Road
Wellingborough
Northamptonshire
NN8 1DH
Tel. 0870 160 3270

CottonTails Rabbit and Guinea Pig Rescue
(Registered charity 1078850)
Sherbourne House
47 Station Road
Westbury
Wiltshire
BA13 3JW
Tel. 01373 864222

Fur & Feather Magazine
Elder House
Chattisham
Ipswich
Suffolk
IP8 3QE
Tel. 01473 652789
www.furandfeather.co.uk

House Rabbit Society
148 Broadway
Richmond
CA 94804
USA
Tel. 001 (510) 970 7575
www.rabbit.org

Rabbit Behaviour Advisory Group
www.rabbitbehaviour.co.uk

Rabbit Rehome
www.rabbitrehome.org.uk

Royal Society Prevention of Cruelty to Animals (RSPCA)
Wilberforce Way
Southwater
Horsham
West Sussex
RH13 9RS
Tel. 0870 33 35 999
www.rspca.org.uk

Rabbit Welfare Association (RWA)
(Registered charity 1085689)
PO Box 603
Horsham
West Sussex
RH13 5WL
Tel. 0870 046 5249
www.rabbitwelfare.co.uk

Society for Companion Animal Studies (SCAS)
The Blue Cross
Shilton Road
Burford
Oxon OX18 4PF
Tel. 01993 825597
www.scas.org.uk

Recommended reading

Brown, M. and Richardson, V. (2000) *Rabbitlopaedia*, Interpet

Davis, S. and Demello, M. (2003) *Stories Rabbits Tell*, Lantern Books

Dykes, L. and Flack, H. (2003) *Living with a House Rabbit*, Interpet

Harriman, M. (1995) *House Rabbit Handbook Third Edition*, Drollery Press

Magnus, E. (2002) *How to Have a Relaxed Rabbit*, Pet Behaviour Centre

McBride, A. (1988) *Rabbits and Hares*, Whittet Books

McBride, A. (1998) *Why Does My Rabbit ...?*, Souvenir Press

Richardson, V. (1999) *Rabbit Nutrition*, Coney Publications

Richardson, V. (2000) *Rabbits: Health, Husbandry & Diseases*, Blackwell Science

Robinson, R. (1978) *Colour Inheritance in Small Livestock*, Fur & Feather

Russell, G. (2004) *Showing Rabbits*, Coney Publications

Sandford, J. (1996) *The Domestic Rabbit, Fifth Edition*, Blackwell Science (out of print)

Thomson, J. (1997) *Gardening with the Enemy*, Janet Thomson

Stockists

Animal Mad
(rabbit accessories, hay racks, medicines, gifts and treats)
19 Pudsey Hall Lane
Canewdon
Essex
SS4 3RY
Tel. 01702 462491
www.animalmad.ltd.uk

Avondale Animal Housing
(rabbit hutches and products including bottle springs)
135 Avondale Road
Stockport
Cheshire
SK3 0WD
Tel. 0161 477 1872
www.avondaleanimalhousing.co.uk

Beaphar
(Xtravital food)
Beaphar UK Ltd
Homefield Road
Haverhill
Suffolk CB9 8QP
Tel. 01440 715700
www.beaphar.com

BunnyBasics.net
(rabbit feeds, toys, treats and accessories)
314 Springvale Industrial Estate
Cmbran
Gwent
NP44 5BR
Tel. 01633 484878
www.bunnybasics.net

Bunny Bazaar
(carriers, treats, feed and health products)
35 St Michaels Crescent
Oldbury
West Midlands
B69 4RT
Tel. 0121 544 1511
www.bunnybazaar.co.uk

Burgess Supafeeds
(Supa Rabbit Excel, Lite and Junior)
PO Box 38
Pickering
YO18 7YH
Tel. 0800 413 969
www.burgesssupafeeds.co.uk

Carr's UK Ltd
(natural health products including Entracare to prevent digestive upsets)
Sheffield Road
Creswell
Worksop
Nottinghamshire
S80 4HN
Tel. 0845 230 9606
www.naturalfeeds.co.uk

Dr Squiggles
(natural health products including Aviclens for bottles)
The Birdcare Company
21–22 Spring Mill Industrial Estate
Avening Road
Nailsworth
Gloucestershire
GL6 0BS
Tel. 0845 130 8600
www.birdcareco.com

The Hay Experts
PO Box 7338
Tadley
RG26 9AW
Tel. 07883 821 099
www.thehayexperts.co.uk

Homes 4 Pets
(rabbit hutches)
The Old Forge Works
Waterloo Street
Harrogate
HG1 5JD
Tel. 01423 701213
www.homes4pets.net

iBreed
(Pedigree and Livestock Management System)
Tel. 07708 429450
www.ibreed.ukgateway.net

John Hopewell Marketing
(Ezi-Filla water bottles, cages and hoppers)
6 Hellaby Lane
Hellaby Industrial Estate

Rotherham
S. Yorkshire
S66 8HN
Tel. 01709 702000
www.johnhopewell.co.uk

Omlet UK Ltd
(rabbit housing and good source of rabbit information)
Tuthill Park
Wardington
Oxon
OX17 1SD
Tel. 0845 450 2056
www.omlet.co.uk

Outdoor Gear UK Ltd
(white judging coats)
72/74 Palmerston Road
Bournemouth
Dorset
BH1 4JT
Tel. 0845 644 3270
www.outdoorgear.co.uk

PetHouse
(rabbit hutches)
Croftons Farm
Rough Hill Complex
The Tye
East Hanningfield
Essex
CM3 8BY
Tel. 01245 401009
www.pethouse-uk.com

PetLife International Ltd
(Oxbow pellets and hay, VetBed)
Western Way
Bury St Edmunds
Suffolk
IP33 3SP
Tel. 01284 761131

Scratch & Newton
(hutch and bottle covers)
First Floor
111–113 New Road Side

Horsforth
Leeds
LS18 4QD
Tel. 0113 259 1117
www.scratchandnewton.com

Supreme Petfoods Ltd
(Science Selective, Russel Rabbit)
Stone Street
Hadleigh
Ipswich
Suffolk IP7 6DN
Tel. 01473 823296
www.russelrabbit.com

Vetark Professional
(multivitamins and probiotics, including AviPro)
PO Box 60
Winchester
SO23 9XN
Tel. 01962 844316
www.vetark.co.uk

West Wales Willows
(Timothy Hay and toys)
Martinique Farm
Wolfscastle
Haverfordwest
Pembrokeshire
SA62 5DY
Tel. 01437 741714
www.westwaleswillows.co.uk

Wilkinsons Pet Bedding
(barn dried hay, straw, wood shavings)
Suttons Farm
Lord Sefton Way
Altcar
Formby
Merseyside
L37 5AA
Tel. 01704 879943
www.wilkinsonspetbedding.co.uk

index

Bridge
Buddhism
Bulgarian
Business Chinese
Business French
Business Japanese
Business Plans
Business Spanish
Business Studies
Buying a Home in France
Buying a Home in Italy
Buying a Home in Portugal
Buying a Home in Spain
C++
Calculus
Calligraphy
Cantonese
Car Buying and Maintenance
Card Games
Catalan
Chess
Chi Kung
Chinese Medicine
Chinese
Christianity
Classical Music
Coaching
Collecting
Computing for the Over 50s
Consulting
Copywriting
Correct English
Counselling
Creative Writing
Cricket
Croatian
Crystal Healing
CVs
Czech
Danish
Decluttering
Desktop Publishing
Detox
Digital Photography
Digital Home Movie Making
Dog Training
Drawing
Dream Interpretation
Dutch
Dutch Conversation
Dutch Dictionary
Dutch Grammar
Eastern Philosophy
Electronics
English as a Foreign Language
English for International Business
English Grammar
English Grammar as a Foreign Language
English Vocabulary
Entrepreneurship
Estonian
Ethics
Excel 2003
Feng Shui
Film Making
Film Studies
Finance for Non-Financial Managers
Finnish
Fitness
Flash 8
Flash MX
Flexible Working
Flirting
Flower Arranging
Franchising
French
French Conversation
French Dictionary
French Grammar
French Phrasebook
French Starter Kit
French Verbs
French Vocabulary
Freud
Gaelic
Gardening
Genetics
Geology
German

German Conversation
German Grammar
German Phrasebook
German Verbs
German Vocabulary
Globalization
Go
Golf
Good Study Skills
Great Sex
Greek
Greek Conversation
Greek Phrasebook
Growing Your Business
Guitar
Gulf Arabic
Hand Reflexology
Hausa
Herbal Medicine
Hieroglyphics
Hindi
Hinduism
Home PC Maintenance and Networking
How to DJ
How to Run a Marathon
How to Win at Casino Games
How to Win at Horse Racing
How to Win at Online Gambling
How to Win at Poker
How to Write a Blockbuster
Human Anatomy & Physiology
Hungarian
Icelandic
Improve Your French
Improve Your German
Improve Your Italian
Improve Your Spanish
Improving Your Employability
Indian Head Massage
Indonesian
Instant French
Instant German
Instant Greek
Instant Italian
Instant Japanese
Instant Portuguese
Instant Russian
Instant Spanish
Irish
Irish Conversation
Irish Grammar
Islam
Italian
Italian Conversation
Italian Grammar
Italian Phrasebook
Italian Starter Kit
Italian Verbs
Italian Vocabulary
Japanese
Japanese Conversation
Java
JavaScript
Jazz
Jewellery Making
Judaism
Jung
Keeping a Rabbit
Keeping Aquarium Fish
Keeping Pigs
Keeping Poultry
Knitting
Korean
Latin American Spanish
Latin
Latin Dictionary
Latin Grammar
Latvian
Letter Writing Skills
Life at 50: For Men
Life at 50: For Women
Life Coaching
Linguistics
LINUX
Lithuanian
Magic
Mahjong
Malay
Managing Stress
Managing Your Own Career
Mandarin Chinese Conversation

Marketing
Marx
Massage
Mathematics
Meditation
Modern China
Modern Hebrew
Modern Persian
Mosaics
Music Theory
Mussolini's Italy
Nazi Germany
Negotiating
Nepali
New Testament Greek
NLP
Norwegian
Norwegian Conversation
Old English
One-Day French
One-Day French – the DVD
One-Day German
One-Day Greek
One-Day Italian
One-Day Portuguese
One-Day Spanish
One-Day Spanish – the DVD
Origami
Owning a Cat
Owning a Horse
Panjabi
PC Networking for Small Businesses
Personal Safety and Self Defence
Philosophy
Philosophy of Mind
Philosophy of Religion
Photography
Photoshop
PHP with MySQL
Physics
Piano
Pilates
Planning Your Wedding
Polish
Polish Conversation
Politics
Portuguese
Portuguese Conversation
Portuguese Grammar
Portuguese Phrasebook
Postmodernism
Pottery
PowerPoint 2003
PR
Project Management
Psychology
Quick Fix French Grammar
Quick Fix German Grammar
Quick Fix Italian Grammar
Quick Fix Spanish Grammar
Quick Fix: Access 2002
Quick Fix: Excel 2000
Quick Fix: Excel 2002
Quick Fix: HTML
Quick Fix: Windows XP
Quick Fix: Word
Quilting
Recruitment
Reflexology
Reiki
Relaxation
Retaining Staff
Romanian
Running Your Own Business
Russian
Russian Conversation
Russian Grammar
Sage Line 50
Sanskrit
Screenwriting
Serbian
Setting Up a Small Business
Shorthand Pitman 2000
Sikhism
Singing
Slovene
Small Business Accounting
Small Business Health Check
Songwriting
Spanish

Spanish Conversation
Spanish Dictionary
Spanish Grammar
Spanish Phrasebook
Spanish Starter Kit
Spanish Verbs
Spanish Vocabulary
Speaking On Special Occasions
Speed Reading
Stalin's Russia
Stand Up Comedy
Statistics
Stop Smoking
Sudoku
Swahili
Swahili Dictionary
Swedish
Swedish Conversation
Tagalog
Tai Chi
Tantric Sex
Tap Dancing
Teaching English as a Foreign Language
Teams & Team Working
Thai
The British Empire
The British Monarchy from Henry VIII
The Cold War
The First World War
The History of Ireland
The Internet
The Kama Sutra
The Middle East Since 1945
The Second World War
Theatre
Time Management
Tracing Your Family History
Training
Travel Writing
Trigonometry
Turkish
Turkish Conversation
Twentieth Century USA
Typing
Ukrainian
Understanding Tax for Small Businesses
Understanding Terrorism
Urdu
Vietnamese
Visual Basic
Volcanoes
Watercolour Painting
Weight Control through Diet & Exercise
Welsh
Welsh Dictionary
Welsh Grammar
Wills & Probate
Windows XP
Wine Tasting
Winning at Job Interviews
Word 2003
World Cultures: China
World Cultures: England
World Cultures: Germany
World Cultures: Italy
World Cultures: Japan
World Cultures: Portugal
World Cultures: Russia
World Cultures: Spain
World Cultures: Wales
World Faiths
Writing a Novel
Writing Crime Fiction
Writing for Children
Writing for Magazines
Writing Poetry
Xhosa
Yiddish
Yoga
Zen
Zulu